BEING CREATIVE INSIDE AND OUTSIDE THE CLASSROOM

# ADVANCES IN CREATIVITY AND GIFTEDNESS

Volume 2

The second book in the Advances in Creativity and Giftedness series creates a level playing field for all those interested in the construct of creativity, but perceive it as being tautological, immeasurable or otherwise obscure. Unlike books that report on studies of creativity using paradigms from psychology or the learning sciences, this book addresses notions such as fluency, flexibility, elaboration and originality for a layman's perspective and makes it accessible to classroom teachers and all those interested in ways of cultivating creativity.

Another refreshing feature of the book is its focus on teaching for creativity by examining the research base on divergent thinking, motivation and creative problem solving. It is my hope that teachers will be able to engage more in developing lesson plans that specifically include cultivatable aspects of creativity after reading this book.

I am pleased to present the second book in the Advances in Creativity and Giftedness series to the community.

**Series Editor:**
  **Bharath Sriraman,** *The University of Montana*

**International Advisory Panel**
  **Don Ambrose,** *Rider University, USA*
  **David Chan,** *The Chinese University of Hong Kong*
  **Anna Craft,** *University of Exeter, UK*
  **Stephen Hegedus,** *University of Massachusetts, Dartmouth*
  **Kristina Juter,** *Kristianstad University College, Sweden*
  **James C. Kaufman,** *California State University at San Bernardino, USA*
  **Kyeonghwa Lee,** *Seoul National University, Korea*
  **Roza Leikin,** *University of Haifa, Israel*
  **Peter Liljedahl,** *Simon Fraser University, Canada*
  **Paula Olszewski-Kubilius,** *Northwestern University, USA*
  **Larisa Shavinina,** *University of Quebec, Canada*

**Editorial Assistant:**
  **Claire Payne**

# Being Creative Inside and Outside the Classroom

How to Boost Your Students' Creativity – And Your Own

*By*

John Baer
*Rider University, USA*

and

James C. Kaufman
*California State University, San Bernardino, USA*

SENSE PUBLISHERS
ROTTERDAM / BOSTON / TAIPEI

A C.I.P. record for this book is available from the Library of Congress.


ISBN 978-94-6091-838-4 (paperback)
ISBN 978-94-6091-839-1 (hardback)
ISBN 978-94-6091-840-7 (e-book)


Published by: Sense Publishers,
P.O. Box 21858, 3001 AW Rotterdam, The Netherlands
https://www.sensepublishers.com/

An earlier version of this book was previously published by Allyn & Bacon under the title *Creative Teachers, Creative Students*.

The "Zero-to-Ten Test of Creativity" on p. 1 was based on the "How Creative Are You?" exercise created by D.J. Treffinger of the Center for Creative Learning.

The "Are Your Ready to Learn CPS?" checklist on p. 94 was adapted from D.J. Treffinger's *Creative Learning and Problem Solving* (Center for Creative Learning, 1986).

The CPS Model of Creative Problem Solving on p. 103 was adapted from S.G. Isaksen & D.J. Treffinger's *Creative Problem Solving: The Basic Course* (Bearly Ltd., 1985).


*Printed on acid-free paper*

# TABLE OF CONTENTS

# PREFACE

This book has two goals. The first is to show you how to teach your students to be more creative thinkers. The second is to help you to develop your own creativity, both in and out of the classroom.

It is not weighted down with detailed discussions of creativity theory or creativity research, although it is based on both. At times one needs to understand a theory in order to put that theory into practice effectively, but in those cases the focus is always on how to *apply* what we know about creativity, not on theory for theory's sake.

This book is designed to be largely self-teaching, and it can be worked through either as part of a course or on one's own. Note the words "work through." There are many activities in the book to help you understand various ideas and techniques. Most of these activities are brief; all are important; and you really shouldn't skip them.

We hope that you find this book interesting, exciting, and just a bit challenging. We are confident that it will help you and your students become more imaginative and more productive thinkers. We also believe that it will help you experience life — all of life — in the most creative and joyous way possible.

We want to thank the many students who have helped us develop and try out the ideas and activities included in this book. Much of what is here was originally created for use in the education classes taught by John, and our students have been generous in sharing ideas about how to refine and improve both the activities themselves and the ways in which we have presented them. In many cases their suggestions have led to significant improvements.

Finally, we would like to thank Roja Dilmore-Rios, Qin Li, and Roderick O'Handley for editorial assistance and David K. Hecht for his outstanding contribution. John wants to thank his daughter, Heather, and his wife, Sylvia, for their inspiration, encouragement, and creativity. Sylvia is the most gifted teacher he has ever known, and many of the ideas and techniques in this book are taken directly from her. Heather has recently become a teacher, joining the profession that her parents love so much. James wants to thank his wife, Allison, his son, Jacob, his parents, Alan and Nadeen, and the rest of his family and friends.

## INTRODUCTION

### *The Zero-to-Ten Test of Creativity*

Let's start with a test of your creativity. Don't get nervous: We just want you to rate your own creativity, in the privacy of your own mind, on a scale of 0-10. A score of 10 is reserved for the most creative people of all time — people like William Shakespeare, Albert Einstein, Emily Dickinson, Claude Monet, and Shikibu Murasaki (author of Japan's — and the world's — first novel, the luxuriantly romantic *Tale of Genji*). We needn't agree on exactly who should be a 10 and who is merely a 9 or a 9.5. It's sufficient that each of us can generate a list of people that we consider creative geniuses, people who can serve to anchor one end of our 0-10 creativity continuum.

Let the other anchor — a rating of zero creativity — be represented by a rock. (And make it a plain, ordinary, and most uninteresting rock, the kind even a geologist couldn't love.)

### THE ZERO-TEN TEST OF CREATIVITY

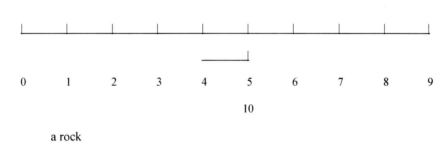

a rock

W. Shakespeare

Think about it for a minute or two: Where on this scale would you rate yourself? None of us is a rock, and none of us is a 10 (at least not yet — generally ratings of 10 are only awarded posthumously!). So where on a 1-10 scale would you put yourself?

You may want to object that it's not that simple, that you can't just give yourself a number that stands for your creativity at all times and in all situations. And you're right: A very reasonable response to this test would probably be something like, "Well, it depends" — and the list of things it depends on is long (infinitely long, no doubt). But even though the *Zero-to-Ten Test of Creativity* is certainly too simple, it does have some redeeming features:

> It makes the point that creativity is a continuum, not something that a person either has in abundance or lacks entirely. We're all creative, to one degree or another, in many of the things we do.

It helps us realize that our creativity varies — from task to task, and even from moment to moment. This is something many psychologists and educators tend forget. (Are you a 6 when painting but only a 4 when cooking? Maybe you're a 3 in the morning and a 7 late at night, or a 5 when you're alone and an 8 when you're with a close friend.)

It can help us become aware of our own tacit understandings of what creativity is. Trying to respond to such a seemingly simple (or perhaps simple-minded!) question pushes us to think about our most basic ideas about what it means to be creative. In doing so, it can help make us aware of the limitations of one-dimensional or single-component conceptions of creative thinking.

> It can help us see the limitations of testing creativity. The *Zero-to-Ten* test is about as valid and reliable as most of the creativity tests on the market — which is to say, not very valid or reliable at all. (It is, however, much easier to take and score.) Be forewarned: We'll be giving you some other creativity "tests" as we go along as ways to introduce or explain new concepts. We think you'll find these tests to be fun to take, but keep in mind that although they will tell us something about creativity, none of them is much more valid as a measure of your overall creativity than the *Zero-to-Ten* test.

Our level of creativity varies for many reasons, and in this book we'll be exploring some of the causes of this variation. We'll also look at ways to get it to vary in a positive direction — to move us, say, from a 4 to a 5, or from a 6 to an 8. And we'll also consider ways to help children be more creative, both in and out of the classroom.

## WHAT IS CREATIVITY?

*The problem of definitions*

That imp-god ambiguity

Giggles at befuddled definers

Who muddle in his double-ended funnel

While fools fall through

Free

This bit of wit is something that one of us found, believe it or not, on a restroom wall. While it may not qualify as great poetry, there is at least a little bit of wisdom in these five lines of graffiti. Certainly in the area of creativity, it is easy to become muddled in definitions and theories. And there may even be times that we might do better *not* to specify exactly what we mean.

Creativity is hard to define, even among psychologists who study it intensively. The fact that psychologists and others cannot agree on a single definition of creativity doesn't mean that we can't study it, however; in fact, one might argue that if it were easy to define, then we would understand it fully and there would be little studying left to do. It is, of course, important that each of us be as careful as possible to specify what we mean when we use the word, so that we can know whether we are talking about the same thing at all. But it's also okay if our definitions allow a little "give," if they provide some room for ambiguity. To use a geographical metaphor, a good definition of a hard-to-define concept like creativity might do better merely to point out the general direction of where one might find it, rather than to try to pinpoint its location precisely on a grid.

## A DEFINITION

As clearly as simply as we can, here is what we mean by the word "creativity":

> Creativity refers to anything someone does in a way that is original to the creator and that is appropriate to the purpose or goal of the creator.

Now we will explain this definition, piece by piece.

*Creativity refers to <u>anything</u>:* When we say that creativity refers to "anything someone does," we mean *anything*. People can be creative in the ways they lay out or weed a garden, write or interpret poems, arrange child-care schedules, plan a vacation, teach multiplication, or play tennis. Creativity isn't limited to a few special, highly valued artistic or scientific activities. Nor is it limited to only a few outstanding ideas or works of art conceived by people who rate at least a 9 on the *Zero-to-Ten* test. We're talking about what we might call "garden variety" creativity, the kind all of us have, use, and enjoy. If you've ever re-arranged your workspace to make it more efficient or pleasant, improved your grandmother's recipe for tuna casserole to make it more even more tasty or more healthful, or figured out a new and workable way to keep telephone salespeople from interrupting you when you're busy, then you've been thinking creatively.

*Creativity refers to anything <u>someone</u> does:* In our definition of creativity, we use the word "someone" intentionally to limit ourselves to *human* creativity. Machines may be able to think or act creatively (today? someday?) — in fact, this is a subject that we personally find quite interesting — but as fascinating as the possibility of computer-generated music or poetry may be, that's not what we're talking about in this book. Nor are we considering the possibility of creative thinking by other (nonhuman) animals, although this may certainly be an interesting thing to ponder!

*Creativity refers to anything someone does in a way that is <u>original to the creator</u>*: By "original to the creator," we mean that it doesn't matter if someone else has already had the same thought, designed a similar gadget, or cooked an identical soufflé. As long as the person who creates is unaware of similar prior creations by others, it qualifies under our definition as creative. (This definition will work for the purposes of this book — to help teachers and parents and students think more creatively — but don't try to use it at the patent office!)

This aspect of the definition doesn't necessarily reflect what scientists may consider creative; indeed, one theory argues that creativity is entirely dependent on the context. In other words, if a novel or piece of art isn't thought to be creative now, then it isn't. If it's thought to be creative one hundred years from now, then it *would* become creative at that time. Although this concept may be reassuring to people who feel like they are unappreciated and misunderstood artists, it's not terribly helpful for trying to improve your own creativity.

*Creativity refers to anything someone does in a way that is original to the creator and that is <u>appropriate to the purpose or goal of the creator</u>*: This means that whatever it is that someone creates, it has to *work*. If a child playing the string game "Cat's Cradle" invents a new way to finger one of the "cradles," it's creative if it works — not if it ends up in a knot. Imagine if you were to hire a company to build a patio for you, and they built it out of rotten salami. Is it different? Absolutely. But simply being original isn't enough. A solution, idea, or painting has to work, and figuring out how well it works depends on one's purpose in creating. This point may seem obvious, but it has often been ignored by psychologists and educators, who have tended to celebrate (and to give high creativity scores to) anything unusual. Sometimes just being different or even weird is fine, in and of itself, but weirdness that *works* is wonderful (and more deserving, we think, of the adjective "creative"!).

Of course, sometimes things "work" in ways we didn't intend, at least consciously. And sometimes our goals change as we go. We don't think we can generally know if a creative idea came as the result of conscious thought, unconscious thought, or serendipity, but we're willing to give credit to the creators of good ideas, even if their creations or their usefulness are somewhat unexpected. Similarly, we don't think there's reason to quibble if someone creates something other than what they set out to create because their goals changed along the way. In *Shakespeare in Love*, we see William Shakespeare working on a new play called *Romeo and Ethel the Pirate's Daughter,* to be filled with swashbuckling adventure. The final product turned out quite different — but still creative. If the creation is meaningful to the creator, then it fits our notion of "appropriate to the purpose or goal of the creator."

This should provide at least a general idea of what we mean when we use the word "creativity." There are many other legitimate ways to think about creativity, of course, such as equating "creativity" with "creative genius," or counting as creative that which is merely unusual, as we just discussed. We don't want to suggest that other definitions are wrong; words can have many different but equally valid definitions. But we want to be clear up front about what we mean when we use the word "creative."

TASK SPECIFICITY

In trying to respond to the *Zero-to-Ten Test of Creativity*, one complaint you might have had was that it depends on the task. Let's use an example from our own lives. John is a much more creative woodworker than he is a cook. He takes risks, tries new designs and techniques, and is often quite playful with the things he might dream up in his shop. In front of the stove, however, he tries to follow directions as closely as possible and becomes uneasy when those directions leave anything to his own judgment (e.g., "Season to taste" or "Boil 8-12 minutes, until tender"). John might be a 6 as a woodworker, but only a 2 as a cook. James is a tremendous baseball fan. When it comes to analyzing baseball statistics and drafting a fantasy team, James is quite creative — and, indeed, can still arrange the data to argue that Phil Niekro (remember him, Braves fans?) was the best pitcher of all time. But James couldn't install an overhead light or nurture a garden or solve a chemistry equation to save his life.

This is common, and the idea that our creativity varies depending on what we are doing seems almost commonsensical. But it's also commonsensical to think that some people are generally "creative types," or that there are some personality traits that make some people more creative whatever they do. Common sense often contains mutually contradictory views, and common sense about creativity is no exception.

In fact, there is much reason to believe that creativity is very task specific. Research has shown that, in general, being creative in one kind of task does not predict how creative a person will be in any other task. It is true that there are some people who are highly creative in many things they do, and there are others who show only minimal creativity across a wide range of activities. But even if creativity on different tasks were distributed completely at random, we would expect to find some people with creative talent in more areas than others. That's how randomness works. If you flip a coin 10 times, and then flip it 10 more times, and then flip it another 10 times, you wouldn't expect to have exactly five heads and five tails in *every* set of 10 flips. Some sets of 10 would probably have more heads, some would more tails. If you made a very large number of flips, of course, you would expect the overall average to be about a roughly even number of heads and tails. And, indeed, a famous statistician named Karl Pearson once flipped a coin 24,000 times and got 12,012 heads — only 12 more than perfectly even! But it would have been completely shocking if every set of his 10 flips had produced an equal number of heads and tails. Similarly, most people have a mixture of higher creativity on some tasks and lower creativity on others, but not everyone has the same total amount of creativity. Our creativity in different tasks is not apportioned equally; rather, it seems that creative talent is distributed pretty much at random.

This is because the skills that underlie creative performance are very task specific. It is not surprising to learn that the skills needed to be a creative mathematician are different from those needed to be a creative metalworker. But the skills needed to be a creative poet do not appear to overlap those needed to be a creative painter. Even two types of creativity that seem to be very related — writing fiction vs. poetry — have their differences. Certainly, both poets and fiction writers are likely to be at least moderately well-read, have a talent for composing words together, and have a fairly rich vocabulary to draw from. Indeed, these talents are important in writing both poetry and fiction, but only because they help provide some of the most basic tools that a writer needs. These basic tools are necessary to achieve even a minimal level of competence as a writer, but neither is very predictive of creative performance once one has reached a modest level of achievement in both. There are plenty of well-read people with rich vocabularies who show little creativity when writing either poetry or short stories — perhaps they are successful journalists, instead. There are many others who evidence more creativity when doing one kind of writing than when doing the other; and there are a (lucky) few who show a great deal of creativity in both kinds of writing. Research has in fact shown that, although some creative poets are also creative short-story writers, this is true only to the degree predicted by chance (assuming similar educational backgrounds). Fundamental or essential skills necessary to perform a task at the most basic level are one part of the picture, but the skills that lead beyond such a basic level of competence to more creative performance tend to be very task specific. This is an idea that we'll return to often throughout this book, but we will give special attention to how we might increase certain task-specific skills in the chapter on divergent thinking (Chapter 2).

We should note that there is some disagreement over whether creative thinking skills are quite narrowly task specific. In fact, there is a lively debate going on regarding this claim, and although we believe the evidence clearly favors task specificity in creativity, it's possible that we are wrong. We have proposed a new model of creativity that reflects task specificity while also allowing for some "general" features. This model is called the Amusement Park Theoretical Model (APT model).

The APT model uses the metaphor of an amusement park. We start with the first level of initial requirements. What do you need in order to go visit an amusement park? Well, just off the top of our heads, you need some money in your pocket, a free day, and a way of getting there. Maybe if you're trying to get to Six Flags or another place filled with roller coasters, you need to be a certain height. Similarly, there are some basic things that you need if you want to be creative. You have to have a basic amount of intelligence — there are few creative carrots. You have to have some level of some type of motivation; few people are creative while lying on a couch, except for those in psychotherapy. And there must be a suitable environment. It is a much different to be creative as a woman in Saudi Arabia versus in California.

Once you have decided to go to an amusement park, you must decide what kind of park you wish to visit. Maybe you are in the mood to go to a water park and splash around. Or perhaps you are feeling more daring and want to ride scary roller coasters that plunge you down rapidly. Maybe you want to see animals or fish, or you want to visit a theme park centered on a cartoon character. Similarly, every aspect of creativity is part of a larger General Thematic Area.

How many General Thematic Areas are there? We're still working on figuring it out. Howard Gardner, in his theory of multiple intelligences, suggests eight areas that seem a reasonable starting point (interpersonal, intrapersonal, spatial, natural history, language, logical-mathematical, bodily-kinesthetic, and musical). Other researchers have suggested different patterns — some of our own work has suggested verbal-artistic, visual-artistic, entrepreneur, interpersonal, math/science, performance, and problem-solving. Shelley Carson and her colleagues used ten domains for their Creativity Achievement Questionnaire: Drama, writing, humor, music, visual arts, dance, invention, science, culinary, and architecture.

Even once you have decided on what type of amusement park to visit, there are still many more decisions left. Even within one area, there are many different parks to choose from. (If you want roller coasters, do you choose Six Flags or Disneyland?) Within each of the General Thematic Areas are several more narrowly defined creativity Domains. Let's say that language is one of the General Thematic Areas. Domains might include journalism, poetry, debate, writing plays, and so on.

Finally, there are the Microdomains. Imagine that you've met the initial requirements of finding an amusement park. You've selected animals as your General Thematic Area, and then narrowed the field down to the Domain of the San Diego Zoo. There are still more choices to make. Do you go see the gorillas? The koala bears? Maybe you want to ride the monorail to get a broad look at all the animals, or go to the souvenir shop and get a tee shirt. Similarly, each Domain has many different Microdomains. Within the Domain of psychology, for example, there's social, developmental, clinical, cognitive, industrial/ organizational, experimental, and so on.

Think of what you consider your most creative area. How specific can you get? What Microdomain might it fall under? How broad can you go? What type of General Thematic Area might include it?

One final point we'd like to make is that even if our model is completely wrong, even if task specificity turns out to be incorrect (no matter whether it is just a little bit wrong or totally wrong), it will do no harm to base your teaching on this idea. Even if you assume creative thinking skills are task-specific and they are, in fact, general, any creativity training or teaching should still work fine. As we will explain in Chapter 2, the only danger is in assuming that creative thinking skills are generic (that is, that they are *not* task specific). If we make *that* assumption and it turns out to be wrong, then we may waste much of our creativity-training effort.

## MOTIVATION

*Why* we do something is almost as important as the skills we bring to the task. We tend to be more creative when doing tasks that we enjoy and find interesting. And on the very same task, our creativity may vary depending on our motivation at the time. When we talk about motivation here, we're being more specific than just meaning "being motivated." We're more interested here in what is sometimes called motivational orientation — what type of motivation drives us? Under conditions of *extrinsic* motivation — such as when we do things for rewards, when we expect our work to be evaluated, or when we are aware of being observed as we work, for example — our creativity decreases. When we are *intrinsically* motivated — that is, when we are doing something for the sheer joy of doing it or simply because we find it interesting — we tend to be more creative.

There are some tasks that are rarely done for fun (or because we are intrinsically motivated). Most people, for example, don't love to file their taxes or scrub their toilets, and their own motivation is extrinsic. Several other tasks are rarely done for any reason *other* than for fun — few people play video games or write poetry for the money involved.

But for many of the things we do — such as writing this chapter — our motivations are mixed and may vary from time to time — sometimes even moment to moment. We may be working away, motivated only by the intrinsic interest of finding ways to put ideas into words that you will understand — and then to receive a call from our publisher, eager to hear how it's coming along. In such an instant, extrinsic motivation zooms up and crowds out any intrinsic motivation... thereby depressing creativity. Unless we do something about it, that is: There are ways to "massage" our own motivations, to get ourselves in a more creative (intrinsically motivated) frame of mind. We'll explore those in some detail in the chapter about motivation.

This isn't to suggest that extrinsic motivation is always bad, however. Sometimes it's the only motivation we have, and it can often keep us going through our less inspired moments when our work seems just like, well, *work*. When John does his woodworking, which he usually enjoys immensely, he sometimes gets tired. James writes plays in his spare times, and often runs smack into writer's block. It's at times like these when John remembers how much his daughter liked the chest he built for her last year, or how much his wife will enjoy the bookcase he's working on right now. It's in these moments that James envisions the audience clapping after one of his plays is performed. Extrinsic motivation is also important for building skills that we might use more creatively some time in the future. In the chapter on motivation we'll consider not only how to increase and maintain intrinsic motivation, but also how to use extrinsic motivation creatively.

## THE JOY OF CREATIVITY

We believe that one of the great joys of being alive comes from thinking creatively, whether that results in a new solution to a problem, an amusing story, a better-running engine, or a tastier soufflé. Even when there is no discernible result — when the soufflé experiment flops, or the innovative idea is one we decide not to pursue — we may nonetheless be engaged in a creative-thinking process that will lead us, in a roundabout way, to a soufflé that is even better than we had hoped, or to an idea that we do choose to develop. Creative thinkers sometimes have to take a long-term perspective; and, in the meantime, the joy of exercising our creative-thinking skills can help make the activities we engage in feel interesting and worthwhile.

It is not the goal of this book to help teachers, parents and students think more creatively for any particular *purpose*. We're not trying to increase the number of Nobel Prizes among our readers, nor are we trying to improve the overall productivity of the U.S. work force. We would be happy if either or both of those things happened, of course (and delighted to think that this book had played some role in such events), but if that's all that happened, we would not have achieved our primary goal.

What we hope to do is to enrich the lives of our readers (and their children and students) by helping them think more creatively — simply because thinking creatively makes us more joyful, more interesting to ourselves and others, more alive to life and its possibilities. If it also helps you (and your children and students) write better poems, cook better soufflés, or solve more challenging problems — and we are sure it will do all these things — these are more on the order of fringe benefits. The primary goal of this book is to provide parents, teachers, and children greater pleasure as the result of becoming more creative thinkers.

Our method will be to tell you briefly some important research findings at the beginning of each chapter and then to show you in some detail how to apply those findings in your life, your home, or your classroom. We won't be giving you long lists of citations of research reports; if you want that, we refer you to the end of each chapter, where we will recommend scholarly books on creativity that should be available in most college libraries. The focus here will be on applications: How to translate research into practice.

## OVERVIEW OF THE BOOK

The rest of this book is divided into four chapters:

### *Divergent Thinking*

Divergent thinking refers to wide array of techniques for coming up with ideas. Brainstorming is the best known of these techniques, but there are many others. This chapter will look at divergent thinking from a task-specific perspective, teach a wide range of techniques for idea generation, and provide a variety of ways of getting "unstuck" when working on seemingly intractable problems.

## *Motivation*

There are many ways to increase students' (and teachers') intrinsic motivation and to help them overcome the negative effects of uncontrollable extrinsic constraints, which will be explained in this chapter and demonstrated using a diverse set of examples. The chapter will also consider the "hidden costs" of rewards and evaluation. Both providing rewards and making evaluations are necessary and often invaluable in many teaching contexts, but they are also known to depress creativity, at least in the short-term. This chapter will help you understand how to use extrinsic motivation to build skills without having a long-term negative impact on the creative use of those skills.

## *Creative Problem Solving Models*

There are several well-respected problem-solving heuristics — general models or guidelines — that can be helpful in solving a wide variety of "real-world" problems. This chapter will explain when and how to use these, teach you the most effective of these models, and explain how to teach this "CPS" model to students.

## CONCLUSION

How do these ideas go together? The final chapter of the book will summarize and tie together the ideas presented in the three main chapters about divergent thinking, motivation, and the CPS model of creative problem solving.

Each of the three main chapters will begin (as did this *Introduction*) with some kind of test as a way to introduce a key idea. A brief discussion of theory will follow, leading up to the heart of the chapter: How to use the idea to help you and your students be more creative.

## BIBLIOGRAPHY

This Introduction touches on many topics that will be discussed in greater detail in later chapters, so we'll save the references related to those specific topics (divergent thinking, motivation, and creative problem solving models) for those chapters.

For a more academic overview of the general topic of creativity, James and Robert Sternberg has collected a very interesting volume of scholarly articles entitled *The Cambridge Handbook of Creativity* (Cambridge University Press, 2010). For those who want to know what is happening on the cutting edge of creativity research, the *Journal of Creative Behavior, Psychology of Aesthetics, Creativity, and the Arts*, and *Creativity Research Journal* are the best sources of up-to-date scholarship on creativity.

If you wish to pursue the idea of task-specific skills, you might try our recent edited book, *Creativity in Different Domains: Faces of the Muse* (Lawrence Erlbaum, 2004), John's book *Creativity and Divergent Thinking: A Task-Specific*

*Approach* (Lawrence Erlbaum, 1993), Robert Sternberg, Elena Grigorenko, and Jerome Singer's *Creativity: From Potential to Realization* (APA, 2004), or Howard Gardner's *Intelligence Reframed: Multiple Intelligences for the 21$^{st}$ Century* (Basic Books, 2000). Gardner's book is a bit easier to read as an introduction to this idea, although his topic is not creativity per se, but thinking of all kinds. Our two books are more technical, but also more up-to-date.

## DIVERGENT THINKING

A QUICK TEST

For this test you'll need a pen or a pencil, plus a watch or some other way to time yourself so you'll know to stop after two minutes. Ready? Here's the task:

List as many different possible uses for empty egg cartons as you can.

(We encourage you not to just skip this "test" and read on. Take two minutes, give it your best effort, and then come back and read what follows.)

CHAPTER 2

You may have heard variations of this kind of task, such as listing uses of bricks, boxes, or tin cans. These are standard creativity test questions. We'll tell you how they're scored later, but first let's give you one more task. For this one you also have two minutes:

    •   List as many different ways as you can to stay cool on a hot day.

(Again, take a moment — just two minutes — and actually write down all the ideas you can think of for how to stay cool on a hot day.)

_____

_____

_____

_____

_____

_____

_____

_____

_____

_____

_____

_____

_____

_____

# CHAPTER 2

Okay, now you have two lists and you want to know how they're scored. Then you'll know how creative you are, right?

Wrong. You already know, if you read Chapter 1, that there's no good way to test creativity, and that includes standard creativity tests. So we're not going to give you a score — it simply wouldn't mean anything. But we will tell you *how* these tests are scored, because the scoring is based on four components or sub-skills, which together make up the skill of divergent thinking. Measuring these component skills doesn't result in reliable creativity test scores, as we'll see, but understanding these four skills will help us learn some important things about creative thinking, and also help us develop our own creative thinking skills. What we're about to tell you about the components of divergent thinking will also allow you to ace most creativity tests, should you ever need to take one. These tests are so unreliable that a few minutes instruction is enough to double or triple most people's scores! Indeed, this is one reason why you won't see these types of tests given along with the SATs and GREs — the College Board and Educational Testing Service spend thousands of dollars to keep their tests from being "coachable." Creativity tests have a long way to go before they could withstand courses designed to improve people's results.

(By the way, if you didn't try either of the two tasks, we encourage you to stop reading for a few minutes and do them. It will help give you a feel for some of what follows, and they're also both good exercises for building some of your creative thinking muscles.)

## A BRIEF HISTORY OF DIVERGENT THINKING AND ITS FOUR COMPONENT SKILLS

### Guilford's Structure of the Intellect Model

Joy P. Guilford first proposed divergent thinking over half a century ago in his "Structure of the Intellect" model. Guilford recognized that thinking is far more complex than the fairly limited set of skills tapped by the intelligence tests of that day (and by many of the tests of *this* day). Guilford's model included 120 different thinking skills in a complex three-dimensional taxonomy of cognitive skills. Guilford's goal was to create a map that would contain — and to some degree explain — all possible varieties of human thought.

A key group of these factors are those he called "divergent production" skills. He believed these skills (which have in more recent years come to be called divergent thinking skills, rather than divergent production skills) are important parts of creative thinking. Divergent thinking is a kind of thinking that aims not at producing correct answers, but rather at coming up with a wide variety of unusual, original, or even off-the-wall ideas.

## Creative genius

There is a great intuitive appeal to the idea that divergent thinking is related to creative thinking. Divergent thinking's goal of producing different, unusual, even bizarre ideas — ideas that "diverge" from the norm — matches the notion many of us share of what creative geniuses are like. Think of the stereotype of a mad scientist, or of a tormented artist who sees a different world than the rest of us (or who marches to the beat of a different drummer, to borrow Thoreau's brilliant metaphor that has now become a cliché). Creativity as madness, or at least as being extremely if not painfully different than the rest of humanity, remains a popular idea in our culture. This stereotype has great staying power, yet the truth is much more mundane. Are creative geniuses "mad"? Sometimes.

Indeed, new research on this topic (some by James) indicates that poets, particularly female poets, are particular prone to mental illness. But many other writers are not particularly likely to be mentally ill, and the results are similarly unclear — and often contradictory — among other artistic professions. Scientific genius, despite images of the "mad scientist," seems to have little relationship to higher-than-average rates of mental illness. The stereotypical image of the mad genius is nowhere near as prevalent in real life, and the actual data are (as is usually the case) more complex than can be summarized in a quick paragraph. Certainly, there is nothing about the mad genius concept that can provide support for a divergent thinking model of creativity.

## Garden-variety creativity

But it's not creative genius we're trying to understand here anyway. Indeed, most creative geniuses don't particularly want to be understood. Our task is to make sense of, and find ways to enhance, the garden-variety creativity of all of us less-than-tens on the Zero-to-Ten Scale. Can divergent thinking help us? It still has an intuitive appeal, even without mad scientist stereotypes. After all, doesn't one need to have an idea that is at least a little bit different to be creative? Certainly divergent thinking must play some role in creative thinking.

## Divergent thinking versus convergent thinking

Divergent thinking is often contrasted to "convergent" thinking, which refers to thinking that focuses (or "converges") on a single correct answer. Convergent thinking is what is measured by most intelligence and achievement tests. Guilford was the first major theorist to argue that divergent thinking — the ability to produce many (not necessarily correct) ideas, to produce unusual and original (but, again, not necessarily workable) ideas, and to take an idea and spin out elaborate variants of the idea — was every bit as important as convergent thinking. Convergent thinking produces correct answers, but divergent thinking produces interesting, imaginative, and potentially creative ideas.

### The Structure of the Intellect Model and divergent thinking today

Guilford's 120-factor model still has its adherents today, but it hasn't exactly revolutionized intelligence testing, which is still based mostly on models using only one or a few convergent thinking factors. One of the few exceptions is the Woodcock-Johnson III, which has a subtest called Ideational Fluency. This subtest, which consists of quickly naming many different things that fit a specific category, is very similar to some of the Torrance Tests. Guilford has influenced many important cognitive theories, however, including Howard Gardner's currently popular theory of "multiple intelligences." Guilford's ideas have also spawned a whole new genre of ability testing.

Because divergent production skills were hypothesized to be important in creative thinking, divergent thinking and creativity gradually became synonymous, and divergent thinking tests came to be called simply creativity tests. Something important is lost, however, when divergent thinking and creativity are confounded. Divergent thinking leads to *potentially* creative ideas, but there's much more to creativity than being unusual or original, as we will see. Indeed, imagine for a moment we ask you to solve a mathematical proof — to demonstrate, let's say, the transitive property — and you write down, "The rain in Spain stays mainly on the plain." Is this unusual? Unquestionably. Is this original? Absolutely. But perhaps a better conception of creativity would also incorporate the concept of whether it addresses the question being asked.

### The components of divergent thinking

Divergent thinking has four components, each of which is typically scored separately on a creativity test:

- *Fluency* refers to the number of different ideas one can produce.

- *Flexibility* refers to the variety among the ideas one produces.

- *Originality* refers to how unusual are the ideas one produces.

- *Elaboration* refers to richness of detail in the ideas one produces.

One's score on test items like the ones that you tried at the beginning of the chapter — listing uses of an egg carton and ways to stay cool — is a sum of the scores received on each of these four dimensions. Having each component contribute to the total score seems reasonable enough, assuming the theory is correct. (More on that later.) But the scoring procedure is actually rigged, unavoidably, in favor of fluency, so that what matters most is simply the number of responses in your list. Let us explain.

*Scoring fluency*

In scoring fluency, there is no check on the appropriateness of the ideas listed. In response to the question about how to stay cool on a hot day, "Standing in front of an air conditioner," "Watching a scary movie that makes you shiver," and "Wearing egg cartons for shoes" each would score one fluency point. It doesn't matter that of these three ideas, one is totally banal and another makes no sense. "Wearing egg cartons for shoes" would neither keep you cool nor be a very useful way to use egg cartons, but it would score one fluency point for either of the two questions (ways to stay cool and ways to use egg cartons). Scoring fluency also ignores the difference between appropriate but banal ideas ("Standing in front of an air conditioner") and more imaginative ideas ("Watching a scary movie that makes you shiver"). It simply makes a raw count of the number of items in the list.

So here's the trick to scoring high on the fluency scale: Write as fast as you can, write as many things as you can, and don't worry if what you're writing really makes any sense. According to the systems for scoring these tests, as long as the ideas are in some marginal way related to the topic, it doesn't matter if they really make any sense. If you're asked to think of different possible uses for a brick, feel free to say "for meatloaf," "to prevent tooth decay," or "as a buffalo." It all counts.

*Scoring flexibility, originality, and elaboration*

But what about flexibility, originality, and elaboration? Scoring these involves fairly complex procedures, but one thing is true of all three: The more ideas you have in your list, the higher your score is likely to be. For example, under originality, the basic scoring idea is to give points to each idea on the list based on the frequency of that idea on the lists of other people who have taken the test. But simply by having many ideas on your list — even not very unusual ones — your score goes up. This is justified theoretically by the notion that a greater *quantity* of ideas should lead to more high *quality* ideas, and there's some truth to that idea. The more ideas one has, the more likely one will have an original, or even a truly creative, idea. Indeed, in real life, according to much research, the best novelists (i.e., the ones who win the most prizes) also tend to be the ones who have written the most novels. The scientists who have the most impact on the field are the ones who produce the most.

But the fact of the matter is that scores on flexibility, originality and elaboration scales correlate so highly with fluency scores that several experts have argued against bothering with the more complicated scoring procedures. It's much easier, and about as accurate, simply to count the number of responses (the fluency score) and let it go at that.

*But if divergent thinking tests aren't good measures of creativity,*
*why is divergent thinking important?*

You now know how to score high on a creativity test, but you also know that scores on these tests really aren't important (unless, of course, you're a fourth grader trying to get into a Talented and Gifted program somewhere, in which case these scores, invalid and easily faked as they are, still play a major role). Is there any *real* value to the idea of divergent thinking?

The answer is yes, there is something important about the idea of divergent thinking, something that will help us both understand creativity better and become more creative thinkers. Divergent thinking tasks, by themselves, do not yield a valid creativity score, and divergent thinking isn't a single skill (or four skills) that can be taught and practiced in one context and then applied in *any* context one encounters, as we will see below. But if we combine the ideas of task specificity and divergent thinking, the result is a powerful new way of thinking about creativity that will help us become more creative thinkers. Understanding divergent thinking and its component parts won't help us *measure* creativity, but they can help us *understand* the nature of creativity and provide us ways to *improve* our creative thinking and that of our students. For that reason, it is worthwhile examining the skills that make up divergent thinking carefully.

*A sample divergent thinking scorecard*

To help you better understand the four divergent thinking skills of fluency, flexibility, originality, and elaboration, it will be helpful for you to see how these are typically scored on a divergent thinking test. It would be both an ethical and a copyright violation to list the exact scoring rules for an actual divergent thinking test item, of course. However, we can give you a general idea of how such items are scored using one of our own divergent thinking questions and creating a scoring system for it like the ones used on actual divergent thinking tests. We'll use the "test" question that you answered at the beginning of this chapter:

List as many different possible uses for empty egg cartons as you can.
  Here is a short list of possible responses:

- storing eggs
- storing a rock collection
- packaging material to keep fragile things from getting crushed
- homes for cockroaches
- homes for honeybees, who could use the 12 egg spaces to create 12 small but connected honeycombs
- shoes for walking on hot sand
- building material for houses
- musical instruments
- kindling to start fires

- place for storing buttons

Now let's score it. (Remember, this is not part of a *real* divergent thinking test, so there are no norms to compare the scores we obtain with anyone else's score.)

### Scoring fluency

Let's start with fluency. There are 10 different responses, so the fluency score is 10. Some of the responses are very similar, like storing eggs, rocks, and buttons, but none are identical, so each counts one fluency point. (If we had listed both "storing rocks" and "storing stones," however, that would only have scored one fluency point.)

### Scoring flexibility

What about flexibility? Here we are looking for different *categories* of responses. Responses 1, 2, and 10 are all about storing things, so that counts one flexibility point; 4 and 5 are about places to live, so that counts another flexibility point; and each other response is in its own category, so that scores five more points for a total of seven flexibility points. For each question on a real divergent thinking test there is typically a list of different categories of responses in the scoring manual to help one score flexibility, but it's generally fairly easy to divide responses into categories even without such a list.

### Scoring originality

To score originality, a real scoring manual would be helpful, because what divergent thinking test developers do is give their test questions to hundreds, or possibly thousands, of people and count how often a particular response is given. (This group of people is called the "norm group.") Then in the scoring manual they list all the responses given by all the people and the frequency of those responses (sort of like the television show "Family Feud," on which people try to guess how often other people respond in certain ways to a question, except that with a divergent thinking test you score more points if you *don't* say what everyone else has said). For example, very common responses like using the egg cartons for storage (numbers 1, 2, and 10 above), to make homes for animals (numbers 4 and 5), or as a packaging material (number 3) might get zero originality points. Using egg cartons for a building material, a musical instrument, or kindling (numbers 7, 8, and 9) might score one originality point each. And using egg cartons for shoes (number 6) might score two originality points. Extra points are awarded for responses that are so unusual that no one in the norm group made such a response.

*Scoring elaboration*

You might have noticed that the response "homes for honeybees, who could use the 12 egg spaces to create 12 small but connected honeycombs" is far more elaborate (and interesting) than the response "homes for cockroaches." This is where elaboration earns points. For each element of elaboration, one elaboration point is scored. The "homes for honeybees" response would score at least two elaboration points, one for "use the 12 egg spaces" and one for "create 12 small but connected honeycombs." The "walking on hot sand" part of the "shoes" response (number 6) would earn one elaboration point, as would the "keep fragile things from getting crushed" part of the "packaging material" response (number 3).

*What do divergent thinking test scores tell us?*

On an actual divergent thinking test, separate scores for fluency, flexibility, originality, and elaboration might be reported, together with a combined divergent thinking score. This score might then be compared to scores earned by others to produce a percentile score that allows you to compare your score to the scores of a large group of others. As you can probably see, knowing the general scoring rules makes it much easier to get a high score, even if the question is not known in advance. Rather than thinking carefully and trying to give only the very best or most interesting responses, one should simply rush to list as many things as possible. The fact that just this little bit of coaching can enable someone to get a much higher score is one reason these test are not very valid.

Another problem with using divergent thinking tests as measures of creativity is that divergent thinking is just one part of creativity. Divergent thinking is an important contributor to creative thinking, but without skill in evaluative thinking — skill in selecting ideas that are actually workable — one is unlikely to produce much that would be considered creative.

Perhaps the biggest problem with divergent thinking tests, however, is the fact that such tests fail to take into account the task specificity of creativity. One might be very creative when it comes to recycling things (something the question about using empty egg cartons in creative ways might measure) but not at all creative when it comes to planning a science experiment, designing a quilt, or writing a play. Because both creativity and divergent thinking appear to be very task specific, skill in divergent thinking on one task is not likely to predict divergent thinking skill on other, very different tasks.

*A task-specific view of divergent thinking*

No one knows where creative ideas come from. As we explained in Chapter 1, the skills that help us think and act more creatively vary greatly from task to task. A person may have a high degree of ability to use many of the skills helpful in writing creative poetry. But this same person may have very few of the skills needed to write a creative short story. (Or, of course, one may have much — or little — talent in both areas.) This is true even within what might ordinarily be thought of as the same "domain" — such as the verbal domain, which would subsume both poetry and story writing, for example. It is also true in other fields, such as the domain of graphic art, or the domain of mathematics. Creativity appears to be task specific.

## *Is creativity task specific?*

In our opinion, yes. As we've indicated earlier, we allow in our Amusement Park Theoretical Model for some general creativity factors. We also want to emphasize that this issue is not close to settled — new research is still being carried out to explore these questions in more detail. There are many respected psychologists who study creativity who would argue with our point of view. But, as we will discuss, past research seems to indicate creativity is domain-specific and — most importantly — we will argue that assuming domain specificity is the safest and most practical course of action.

Research has repeatedly demonstrated that creative performance in one kind of task within a given domain is often not predictive of creativity on other tasks in the same domain. Typical studies ask people to produce two or more different products (such as poems, descriptions of pictures, and short stories; or sketches, clay sculptures, and collages) and then examine if the people who are creative on one task are more or less likely to be creative on other tasks. When the various products are given to expert judges to rate for creativity, two interesting results consistently emerge. First, the judges, even though they work totally independently of one another, tend to agree to a remarkable degree on the creativity scores they give. (For those of you who like to attach numbers to things, the inter-rater reliabilities are generally in the .75 to .95 range.) Second, the scores achieved by individuals on different tasks vary widely. (The judges, of course, do not know who made which product. Products are identified only by numbers, which are coded so that only the experimenter can match the various products created by a single individual.)

Knowing a person's creativity "score" on one task does not help us predict that person's score on other tasks — even tasks within the same general domain. It does help us predict creative performance in the future on the same kind of task, however. The people in any group who write the most creative poems this year are generally the same ones who will write the most creative poems if tested again a year later. This trend makes sense; indeed, most abilities that involve intelligence or thinking tend to remain consistent over time.

Research has also shown that if a student is trained on focused divergent thinking activities, the benefits are usually quite narrow — the student will only improve on those specific activities. On the other hand, divergent thinking training that uses a wide range of topics in its training exercises produces a much more general improvement in creative performance. In the latter case, the magnitude of the improvement may not be as great as in the case of narrowly targeted training, but it influences performances across a wide range of task domains.

This task specificity of creative performance is true of young children, and it's also true of adults. The only limitation on this generalization is that in some domains, a certain level of training, skill, or knowledge may be necessary to do *any* of the tasks in that domain. Imagine, for example, trying to perform any level of neurosurgery with no prior experience! Still, among those with that prerequisite level of skill or knowledge, creativity on different tasks in the domain is usually randomly distributed.

Although we don't know exactly what these creativity-relevant skills might be for any particular task, divergent thinking theory gives us an important clue, at least when we are talking about the everyday "garden variety" creativity that we all share. The four components of divergent thinking, when considered as task-specific skills, are very useful tools in understanding and promoting creative thinking. We should note that what follows may, or may not, apply to genius-level creativity. We simply don't know, although it's a good guess to assume that it applies in those special cases as well.

### Why it is wise to assume that creative thinking skills are task specific

Unless one is *absolutely* sure that creative thinking skills (like divergent thinking) are *not* task specific, it makes sense for teachers or anyone who wants to improve their creativity to assume they are. We're not saying this just because we believe the evidence for task specificity is stronger than the evidence for more generic creative thinking skills. Even if one thinks that it is likely that creative thinking skills are more generic than task specific, it makes sense to act as if the task specificity hypothesis is the correct one. Let us explain why. (Let us also say that this is somewhat complicated, and if you don't need to be convinced, nothing will be lost by skipping ahead to the next section on *Nurturing task specific divergent thinking skills*.)

The basic idea is this: Even if the task specificity hypothesis is wrong, *nothing* will be lost by basing your creativity training on that assumption. If the task specificity hypothesis is correct, however, and you base your training on the assumption that divergent thinking skills on one task *will* transfer to any other creativity-relevant task, then much of your effort to improve your (or your students') divergent thinking skills may be wasted. We will give two examples to clarify this point.

> *Example 1*: Suppose you want to improve your divergent thinking skill on a wide variety of tasks. The task specificity hypothesis would lead you to practice divergent thinking using a wide variety of tasks (let's say, computer programming and writing poems and building model airplanes). In contrast, under the generic divergent thinking hypothesis it wouldn't matter what tasks you used. They could all be very similar in content (such as writing haikus and sonnets and limericks).

The result is that if the generic hypothesis is correct, then the content of the exercises one uses doesn't matter and nothing is lost by making the incorrect (task specificity) assumption. Maybe you've done a little more work than you had to do, but nothing worse.  But if the task specificity hypothesis is correct and you choose all exercises from the same task domain (which the generic hypothesis allows you to do), then the loss will be significant, as any improvement in divergent thinking will be limited to the single task domain from which the exercises are chosen.  So in our example above, your improvement would be limited to writing poetry.

> *Example 2*:  In contrast to Example 1, let's say that you wish to improve divergent thinking on one single narrowly defined task — for example, cooking.  The task specificity hypothesis would lead you to choose many exercises within this one task domain — baking bread, grilling shrimp, sautéing vegetables, scrambling eggs, etc. The generic hypothesis, in contrast, argues that it doesn't matter what kinds of divergent thinking exercises you choose.  You could improve your divergent thinking in teaching your dog to sit or inventing a children's toy.  Again, the penalty for being wrong is negligible for the task specificity hypothesis, but potentially large for the generic hypothesis.

We hope this makes it clear that, although the question of task specificity in creativity is still unresolved, it nonetheless makes sense (until there is such resolution) simply to adopt the task specificity approach.  Creative thinking often involves working under a cloud (or a rainbow!) of ambiguity.  Although we're fairly confident that further research and expert opinion will continue to move the field of creativity in the direction of task specificity, we'd argue that the question doesn't have to be fully answered.  You can go ahead with your creativity training with full confidence that your efforts will not be wasted.

### *Nurturing task specific divergent thinking skills to increase creativity*

To increase your divergent thinking skill (and your creativity) on a particular task, you should concentrate your practice on things that relate in some way to that task. For example, if you are only interested in improving your creativity (or your students' creativity) in the area of graphic design, then you should do lots of divergent thinking practice using graphic design questions and materials.  But if you are interested in improving your creative thinking skills in general, then you should use a wide range of divergent thinking exercises covering many diverse topics.

We'll be looking somewhat intensively at three examples of areas in which one might want to be more creative:  poetry writing, graphic arts, and a geography activity.  There's nothing special about these topics — almost any topic could be used — but we hope they provide a sense of the range of ways one might practice divergent thinking.

Because we want to indicate how one might target divergent thinking activities in a single domain, we have looked at several abilities related to each of the three examples.  In your classroom, you will often be far more opportunistic in your choices of divergent thinking topics, using both topics that relate directly to what you are studying and choosing topics just for fun.  One common divergent thinking activity is to have students list anything they know (or think they know) about a topic they are about to study.  This can serve at least three purposes:  activating students' prior knowledge about a topic, providing a quick assessment of what they know and don't know about the topic, and developing their divergent thinking skills in an area of interest.

In a sense, we will be starting with more difficult examples — difficult because we have tried to identify specific divergent thinking skills that relate to three particular abilities of interest — and then moving on to some easier examples (which we'll provide in a list of topics at the end of the chapter). Divergent thinking needn't be targeted at a specific ability, as we have done in the three examples we'll be using for the next several pages, nor must it have any particular goal. Almost any divergent thinking activity has the potential to enhance creative thinking in some domain, even if it isn't readily apparent what that domain might be. To give a simple example, one might practice divergent thinking by making a list of words that include the letter "v," or a list of three-syllable words that *don't* include the letter "e." What kind of creativity might that improve? Well, it might make one better at games like Scrabble. Or one might do what one author did and structure an entire novel — more than 300 pages — around the idea of writing without using the letter "e"! (This "e"-free book was originally published in German, and then a translator used the same no "e" rule for the English-language version. In an essay about the monumentally difficult task the author of this book and its translator had taken on, a *New York Times* book reviewer discussed the idea of having freedom within constraints, much as a poet might choose to be constrained artificially by conventions of rhyme or meter. But writing without the letter "e"? What a severe constraint to put on one's self!)

We hope the three examples that follow provide a sense of ways divergent thinking skills can be developed in a variety of domains. These are only examples, however, not prescriptions for the way you should teach divergent thinking in your classroom or practice it yourself. The topics you choose for divergent thinking practice should fit your interests and those of your students. They should relate to the kinds of abilities you want your students to develop and that you want to develop yourself. And they should be the kinds of activities that you and your students find fun and challenging.

## *Example 1: Creativity in writing poetry*

Let's start with an example. Suppose you want to be a more creative poet. What are some of the skills that a poet might need? Here are a few abilities that we think would help:

Creating interesting and meaningful metaphors

Thinking of words that have identical ending sounds/ (rhyme), similar ending sounds (assonance), or identical initial sounds (alliteration)

Forming rich images that suggest many different things

Having ideas and thoughts that can have an effect on other people

This certainly is only a beginning, and depending on the kind of poetry you want to write, the list would change (and might not include even some of the things on this list at all; people who want to write Haikus will not need rhyming skill). But it will serve as an example.

Let's start with alliterative skill because it's rather easy. If you want to improve a skill, it makes sense to practice it. (Practice doesn't make perfect — at least not for most skills, in which perfection is a rather fuzzy concept anyway — but it will still help.) How might one practice to improve skill at alliteration?

Here's where what we know about divergent thinking comes in. The first thing we would want to do is to increase fluency. To do this, you could practice things like generating lists of words that begin with specific sounds. You might choose words randomly (e.g., by opening a book and pointing, or by picking a word from a billboard one passes) and then try to think of as many words as you can with the same initial sound. This is something you can do anywhere, like when you're stuck in traffic or waiting in line at the checkout counter (e.g., "check-out, champion, cheese, chase, choosy, Cheshire, cheek, chin, Czechoslovakia, China, chair, chariot, cheetah …").

Fluency in alliterative skill is a start. What about flexibility, originality, and elaboration? To improve flexibility, you could set yourself the task of thinking of very different *kinds* of alliterative words, such as allowing yourself only one word in a given category (in the example for the previous paragraph, you wouldn't allow both "cheek and chin" or "Czechoslovakia or China"). Or you might specify a rule about the numbers of syllables in the words, such as all three-syllable words, or specify that each word must have either one more or one fewer syllable than the preceding word.

Perhaps more interesting in the case of alliteration, you might strive for originality — searching for words that few others would think of. In the list of words starting with "check-out," "Czechoslovakia" is perhaps most unusual simply because it doesn't start with the same two letters as the others, and "chinaberry" would have been a more unusual word for this list than "China" simply because fewer people would tend to think of it. There's not a specific rule in this case, only a reminder to one's self to look for unusual, original words.

Elaboration? You might simply strive for it (not simply "cheese," but "cheese beginning to develop age spots"). Or you might try some combinations, such as "chasing a cheetah in a chariot."

The point is that, although there's not a generic skill of divergent thinking that will help you be more creative *whatever* you do, there are many task specific divergent thinking skills that one can improve. Just as we can think of exercises to help us become more adept at alliteration, so we can with other skills that matter to us, such as finding metaphors or creating rich images. We'll give some examples for these two skills in a moment, but first let's look at two other examples — improving divergent thinking in graphic arts and in a geography activity.

*Example 2: Creativity in graphic arts*

Suppose you want to improve your divergent thinking skills in the area of graphic arts. First you need to think of some skills that might contribute to creativity in this field. Here are three:

1.  Ability to think of interesting ways to make use of a particular graphic element

2.  Ability to think of interesting ways to represent a given object or idea using different graphic elements

3.  Ability to use color and/or texture to suggest different moods or feelings

If you're a graphic artist it will be easy for you to generate a long list of such skills — in fact, it would be an interesting divergent thinking exercise to do so — but for our purposes this short list will give an idea of some of the kinds of divergent thinking skills we might want to practice.

Let's use the first idea on our list, the ability to think of interesting ways to make use of a particular graphic element. Fluency is generally the best place to start. Can you think how to improve fluency skills in this area?

Here's one exercise that should help: Give students (or yourself) sheets of paper with a half dozen circles spaced around each page. Ask them to use each circle as the basis of a different sketch. For example, on one page they might turn the circles into a face, the wheel of a car, one ring of the Olympics symbol, part of a bull's eye, a basketball, and the wheel of a bicycle. In each case they would make a sketch of the whole thing, with the circle becoming one part of their drawing.

Can you see how to increase flexibility? You might encourage them to make every sketch of a different kind of object. In the example above, you wouldn't want both a car wheel and a bicycle wheel.

How about originality? This time, suggest that they try to think of things that no one else would be likely to think of. In the example above, most of the ideas are probably fairly common. For originality you might try something like turning the circle into the opening of a birdhouse or a doorknob or a television test pattern.

Elaboration in this case might involve either including more details in one's sketches or including other elements in them. In our drawing of a birdhouse, for example, we might draw a perch for the birds, shading on the roof, or the grain of the wood. Or we might include the (human) house the birdhouse is attached to, or birds flying in the vicinity, or trees or other landscape elements. To get students to practice elaboration, you might explain it and then simply encourage it.

These four divergent thinking skills are not mutually exclusive and they needn't be practiced separately. Once you and your students become accustomed to using them, it will probably become natural to try for all four at the same time. At first, however, it generally makes sense to start with fluency and then to emphasize each of the others in turn, rather than to introduce them all at once and risk confusing students or letting some of the four skills be neglected. And even after your students become quite comfortable with all four, they will still need to be reminded now and then to try for all of them.

*Example 3: Creativity in a geography project*

This example relates to a particular assignment that one of us (John) has used in sixth- and seventh-grade geography classes. The project was to create a continent somewhere on the globe and to explain how it might have developed. The general goal was to help students understand how geography and human history interact — how land forms, weather, waterways, etc. influence the things people do and how they do them, and how the things people do and the ways they do them might be adapted to differing geographical settings.

John also wanted to use the activity as a way to encourage students' creativity. And to that end, he started off with some exercises designed to improve some divergent thinking skills that might be used in the project. Here are three abilities that he thought might help them make their projects more creative:

Ability to think of specific cultural elements that might be influenced by geography

Ability to think of ways that geography might influence general features of a culture

Ability to think of ways that a people's culture might lead them to adapt different geographical elements to a given purpose

Let's use the first item on this list, ability to think of specific cultural elements that might be influenced by geography, and see if we can find ways to improve students' divergent thinking skills in this area.

Again, we would start with fluency, but perhaps more than the previous two examples we first need to discuss the context in which these activities would be carried out. If the class had been working on the relationship between geography and culture already and understands the term "cultural elements," then the task we give them can be fairly straightforward. The exercise might be something like, "Think of as many different cultural elements that might be influenced by geography as you can."

But if we're using this as an introductory activity — which is a great way to use divergent thinking, both to practice the skill and to get a sense of what students know — then we first need to explain a bit about what "cultural elements" are, and perhaps give a few examples of how these might be influenced by geography (e.g., how transportation might be influenced by rivers or mountains, how clothing might be influenced by climate, and how diet might be influenced by both climate and topography, to name a few easy ones). Students might note that almost any part of a culture, even its attitudes toward education or its marriage institutions, could be influenced by its geography, and that's fine. Then the activity becomes the same as listing as many cultural elements as one can think of. In fact, you might want to start with this question as soon as you explain what you mean by "cultural elements."

We hope it's clear that there are not right and wrong ways to do this, or right and wrong divergent thinking tasks. You adapt the activities to meet the needs of your students, both in terms of what they know and in terms of their understanding of divergent thinking.

We said we would start with fluency. This is easiest and it allows students to get involved in the activity most quickly. It also allows the teacher to assess students' understanding of the concept of cultural elements and how they might be influenced by geography. To push for flexibility, one simply needs to encourage students to look for different *kinds* of ideas (they might, for example, unnecessarily limit themselves to aspects of material culture, ignoring social relations, customs, ideas, methods of child-rearing, etc.). To encourage originality, one might ask students to try to think of unusual ideas, or ones that few other people would think of. And you might try asking follow-up questions and encouraging full, detailed answers to practice elaboration.

We will go back to each of these three examples (poetry, graphic arts, and geography) to consider ways to encourage divergent thinking in the abilities we haven't looked at yet, but first we should stop for a moment to discuss brainstorming — a much-misunderstood activity.

### Brainstorming

Brainstorming is the most widely used, and probably most powerful, divergent thinking tool available. Brainstorming has become such a commonly used word that it comes as a surprise to many people that brainstorming isn't something that slowly evolved, or was just always there, as is typical with other kinds of thinking such as classifying or summarizing. Brainstorming was invented by one person — his name was Alex Osborn — at a particular time (the 1950s) and place (Madison Avenue in New York City, where Osborn worked in advertising). Osborn invented brainstorming as a way of increasing the number of good ideas a group of people could produce.

The purpose of brainstorming is to produce divergent thinking. In fact, many people think of brainstorming and divergent thinking as the same thing, but that's not really true. Brainstorming is a technique, a method, a means to an end; divergent thinking describes a kind of thinking, and is not a means but an end in itself. And yet the two are very closely related.

Brainstorming helps *produce* the kind of thinking we call divergent thinking, but to say they are the same would be like saying communication and talking are the same. Talking is one way to communicate, but despite this connection, the two terms "talking" and "communication" refer to different things. In the same way, brainstorming and divergent thinking refer to different things. Brainstorming is *one* way — probably the most important way — to produce divergent thinking, but it isn't the only way, as we will see. And using brainstorming doesn't guarantee that one will succeed in producing divergent thinking. One can follow the rules of brainstorming without engaging in divergent thinking, just as one can talk without succeeding in communicating. If done well, however, both talking and brainstorming will produce their desired outcomes.

There are explicit rules for brainstorming, which is another way brainstorming differs from most thinking skills. Brainstorming is *not* just a bunch of people sitting around thinking great thoughts or saying whatever comes to mind. Here is the most important rule:

- Defer judgment.

In brainstorming, the goal is to produce a large *quantity* of ideas without regard to the *quality* of ideas. (This should sound like fluency.) Judging the quality of ideas is not considered in any way unimportant; it is simply deferred, not abandoned entirely. It comes later, as a separate step in the process of developing ideas.

### *Why defer judgment?*

There's good reason for this. Imagine being in a group of people that is trying to come up with ideas. Someone suggests something — perhaps it's you, perhaps someone else — and the idea is greeted with comments like "That will never work," "What a dumb idea!" and the like. After hearing this kind of criticism, are you more or less likely to take a risk by suggesting another idea that might be a little different?

Most people understand this — not that it stops them from being instant critics, because that's something we all seem to love to do — and they assume that deferring judgment means not criticizing. But deferring judgment means postponing both negative *and* positive feedback: No criticism and no praise.

Why no praise?, you might wonder. That should certainly encourage people. But does it? Imagine yourself back in that group, and someone (not you) suggests an idea. Immediately people begin to say what a great idea it is; they might say things like "That's the best idea yet" or "Brilliant idea!" What effect does that have on you and the somewhat offbeat, not-well-formed idea that is just then coming into your mind?

If you're like most of us, it leads you to compare your idea to the "brilliant idea" you just heard praised. That is, it leads you to *judge* your idea, something you want to avoid.

Not that we can ever totally turn off our own critical judgment of our own ideas, or those of others. But Osborn believed that the less judging of ideas early on, the more likely it would be that truly original, unusual, interesting ideas would eventually emerge. Quantity leads to quality.

### *Brainstorming rules*

There are other rules to brainstorming, although different authors may give you slightly different sets of rules. What follows is a representative list of the rules of brainstorming — a full list, including the one rule that we already talked about.

- Defer judgment.

- Avoid ownership of ideas. When people feel that an idea is "theirs," egos can get in the way of creative thinking. They are likely to be more defensive later when ideas are critiqued, and they are less willing to allow their ideas to be modified.

- Feel free to "hitchhike" on other ideas. This means that it's okay to borrow elements from ideas already on the table, or to make slight modifications of ideas already suggested.

- Wild ideas are encouraged. Impossible, totally unworkable ideas may lead someone to think of other, more possible, more workable ideas. It's easier to take a wildly imaginative bad idea and tone it down to fit the constraints of reality than to take a boring bad idea and make it interesting enough to be worth thinking about.

When you brainstorm all by yourself, it's often called "brainwriting." Either way, it's important to keep a written record of all ideas. The best ideas won't automatically float back into consciousness when it's time to critically appraise the results of brainstorming.

How long should brainstorming continue before allowing judgments of ideas? It depends on the situation. Brainstorming is less practical when you're under strict time constraints (indeed, it may be best not to brainstorm for solutions when you have to defuse a bomb). The best ideas often come only later, after the obvious ideas have been suggested, and often after it seems like the group's (or individual's) imagination has run dry. In general, the longer the better, but sometimes a few minutes is all the time you have, or all the time you're willing to spend on a particular problem or issue.

Brainstorming will come up again and again in this chapter and in the one on Creative Problem Solving. It is *not* the only idea-generation technique that's been invented, although it is the one used most frequently. Later in this chapter we'll introduce you to some other ways to generate ideas for particular purposes, but for right now, brainstorming will be the tool we will use to produce divergent thinking. Let's see how to apply it in different situations.

*Using brainstorming to improve skill in creating verbal metaphors*

A few pages ago we produced this short list of skills that would help one write more creative poetry:

Creating interesting and meaningful metaphors

Thinking of words that have identical ending sounds/ (rhyme), similar ending sounds (assonance), or identical initial sounds (alliteration)

Forming rich images that suggest many different things

Having ideas and thoughts that can have an effect on other people

We explained above how to increase one's divergent thinking alliterative skills, and we trust that you can stretch these same ideas to create your own exercises for improving divergent thinking rhyming and assonance skills. Let's try the other three — thinking of interesting metaphors, rich images, and ideas that can affect other people — to develop some different kinds of divergent thinking exercises. We'll start with metaphors.

### *What are metaphors?*

Metaphors are words or phrases that suggest a similarity between things or actions that we normally think of as unrelated. You can't really drown in sorrow, or money (although you can drown in chocolate syrup, so don't try it). A highway isn't really a thin blue ribbon unraveling to the horizon, and even in the very worst of storms it never really rains cats and dogs. Being tickled pink is generally only a figure of speech (describing a feeling that involves neither tickling nor the color pink). But metaphorically they work to express something that more ordinary words might miss. By the way, for the English teachers among you, we're going to use the word "metaphor" to refer to both true metaphors, like the examples we've just given, and similes, such as "the sand was as hot as a firewalker's coals" or "the rain was like a percussion section practicing on the roof."

Another disclaimer about our use of the term "metaphor": Many kinds of comparisons are metaphorical in nature — in fact, some people have argued that all thinking and learning is deeply metaphorical — but we are referring to metaphors in a much more restricted sense. The goal here is to use divergent thinking to help create interesting verbal metaphors. Metaphorical thinking in a much broader sense is sometimes thought of as a skill underlying divergent thinking, but confusing these two meanings of "metaphor" can make all of this seem very circular (i.e., metaphorical thinking leads to divergent thinking, which in turn leads to making metaphors.) The problem is that that the term "metaphor" has many different and rich meanings. (Can you think of any word more suitable to having many different meanings than "metaphor"?)

### *Where do metaphors come from?*

The source of metaphors is as puzzling as the many meanings of the word. Sometimes they're borrowed — and when they have been borrowed and repeated many times, we call them clichés. But where do original metaphors come from?

No one really knows. There has been some ingenious research on how we *understand* metaphors, which is a rather tricky business in itself. Think about it: How is it that we know when a poet says that "tiny orange and red flags fluttered from the tree like crumpled confetti" she is talking about autumn leaves, not

Spanish flags or little bits of paper? And *understanding* metaphors is, for most of us, the easy part. Inventing new ones is a far greater challenge.

We're not going to tell you how we do it because we don't know how we do it. At some level it certainly involves synapses in the brain and neurotransmitters of one kind of another; at another level it must involve one's knowledge of the world and of words; and at yet another (more metaphorical) level it probably involves a certain degree of (largely unconscious) cognitive playfulness. But no one knows the formula for brewing original metaphors; at best we understand small pieces of the puzzle.

### Improving metaphor-making skills

Not knowing exactly how metaphors are produced doesn't mean we can't improve our metaphor-making skills, however. We don't know how to grow muscle tissue in our biceps either, and yet we know what kinds of exercises will cause those muscles to grow. Fortunately, the same is true of your "metaphor muscle." There are exercises that will cause it to become stronger, more active, and generally better — and disuse will lead it to atrophy. The key to increasing the strength of this "metaphor muscle" is applying the principles of divergent thinking (via the practice of brainstorming and other idea-generation techniques) to metaphor production.

Here's one way to do just that. Think of an object, or a feeling; for simplicity, let's start with a computer screen. What else could the computer screen be called? An eye, a chalkboard, an intermediary between me and a computer brain, a Ouija board, a page from a book, a swimming pool with letters floating on its surface, a taskmaster, a flickering goddess . . . This is brainstorming, so remember: There are no right or wrong answers, we're looking for a large quantity of ideas, and we'll concentrate on quality later.

For something that is as hard for most of us as coming up with metaphors, it probably makes sense to work for a while simply on fluency. If you know the kind of poetry you want to write, use words or ideas from that realm as your starting point and brainstorm metaphors for those words or ideas. As you get more fluent, when it becomes easy to generate a stream of 10 or 20 metaphors for almost anything, then shift your focus a bit to work on flexibility, originality, and elaboration. For flexibility, you might try to make each idea as independent of the previous ones on your list as possible (thus over-riding the "Feel free to 'hitchhike'" rule of brainstorming). For originality, try to think of metaphors that no one else would think of. And for elaboration, try to put each metaphor that you think of in a different context, and add the kinds of details that make it richer, fuller, and more descriptive. You might find yourself with a whole lot of poem fragments which later — after brainstorming, when you turn your critical judgment back on — you might want to develop into poems, or save for use another day.

Here are some examples to get you started:

The moon …

A flat tire when you're late for work …

A puppy …

A penny on the ground …

Envy …

A sudden sneeze …

*Using brainstorming to improve skill in creating rich verbal images*

We hope that the basic technique behind all of these examples is becoming clear. Let's try another example in the domain of writing poetry: In what ways might we improve our "Ability to think of rich images that suggest many different things"?

First we need to have some idea what "images" means. Images are a kind of mental picture, but here we're referring to words that conjure up an image. Images can also be thought of as extended metaphors; in fact, some people would say that they are not two distinctly different things, and to an extent we would agree. But there is something more precise about a metaphor: In a metaphor, there is something being compared in some way to something else. Images are often more loose, and they may go off in many different directions. For example, a description of a frog jumping into a still pond may suggest many different things without being a metaphor for any particular thing, idea or action.

What we're talking about when we use the word "images" is a description that evokes a mental picture, and the kind of image we're looking for is one that is at the same time clear and also suggestive of other things, ideas, moods, actions, times, places, etc. Sometimes poets want to nail down an image, to tell exactly what something is like, and at other times they use images to suggest other things. It is the latter class of images that we're talking about.

How can we improve our skill at generating interesting, rich, suggestive images? You've probably guessed it already: We practice brainstorming the kinds of images we want to be better able to produce. Poets often keep notebooks in which they jot down images that they might use later in poems. If, like us, images don't come to you, unbidden, on a regular basis from some generous muse, then you might try brainstorming images — any images at all at first. As this becomes easier, you might put some kinds of constraints on the kinds of images you're looking for. You might search for different kinds of images (not all pastoral ones, for example, or all ones that include people, or animals, or buildings, or whatever comes to your mind all too readily) in an effort to improve the flexibility of your image-creating skill. You might search for unusual, highly original images; or you might take time to elaborate each image into a full and richly evocative scene.

*Using brainstorming to generate ideas and thoughts that can have an
effect on other people*

By now you probably can guess what we're going to suggest as a method to
improve one's divergent thinking in the area of generating affecting ideas. The
particular brainstorming task might depend very much on the context, of course. If
one already has a topic in mind for a poem, the range of possible ideas would be
somewhat narrowed, but whether one has a narrow or wide focus, simply trying to
list many ideas as possible that might have an effect on other people, then pushing
for varied and unusual ideas of this kind would help develop one's divergent
thinking ability in this area. (It might also give you a long list of topics for poems.)

Poetry was just one of the three examples discussed earlier in this chapter. Let's
turn to the second example, graphic art, and see how to employ brainstorming to
improve divergent thinking skills in that domain.

*Using brainstorming to improve skill in representing an object using
different graphic design elements*

In discussing creativity in graphic art, we listed three skills that might help make
one a more creative graphic artist. The three skills were:

Ability to think of interesting ways to make use of a particular graphic element

Ability to think of interesting ways to represent a given object or idea using different
graphic elements

Ability to use color and/or texture to suggest different moods or feelings

We already looked at the first one, so let's try the other two, using brainstorming as
our tool. We'll start with the ability to think of interesting ways to represent a
given object or idea using different graphic elements. As before, we're aiming this
example at students, not graphic artists (who might find these exercises a bit too
elementary).

You could provide a set of graphic elements — these could be as simple as
some geometric shapes, or they might include very complex shapes or designs —
and have students brainstorm different ways these pieces might be used to
represent some object, such as the human body, or a building, or a flower. Because
this activity would in all likelihood involve either arranging a set of graphic
elements or sketching them on paper, this would probably be something students
would do individually, not as a group. It is therefore not actually brainstorming,
but more like brainwriting (or perhaps we should call it "braindrawing"?).

As always we recommend stressing fluency first; for many students, this will be
difficult enough without additional constraints such as trying to come up with
unusual or elaborate designs. If your students become adept at this kind of
exercise, however, you might want to encourage flexibility, originality, or

elaboration, especially if they seem to be coming up with the same kinds of ideas again and again.

Here are some examples of what we mean:

- ₪
- $\partial$
- §
- ¥
- ⊙
- ⌘
- ℵ

*Using brainstorming to improve skill in using color and texture to suggest different moods or feelings*

Hopefully by now you're getting the idea, so perhaps you can guess the kind of brainstorming activity we're going to suggest. Of course, there isn't just one way to do this, so you might come up with a brainstorming activity that is very different from this activity but every bit as good.

Here's something you might do. First have students brainstorm different moods or different feelings (envy, joy, disgruntlement, etc.). Then choose one mood or feeling and have them brainstorm ways to use color (or texture) to evoke that mood or feeling. You could have them do this only using words to describe how they envision doing it graphically, but it might also be interesting to have students use some media (such as colored pencils, crayons, or paints) to create the mood using only colors (that is, without any representational drawings). But make sure to instruct them to try to think of many *different* ways to do it, not to think of just one and work only on that. Students might all work on the same mood or feeling, or on different ones.

The third example used earlier in this chapter was from a geography project. Let's see how brainstorming might help there.

*Using brainstorming to think of ways geography might influence culture*

The three skills we listed that might enhance creativity on this geography project were:

Ability to think of specific cultural elements that might be influenced by geography

Ability to think of ways that geography might influence general features of a culture

Ability to think of ways that a people's culture might lead them to adapt different geographical elements to a given purpose

We've already looked at how to improve divergent thinking skills for the first geography ability, so let's work on the second one:.

*Using brainstorming to think of ways that geography might influence
general features of a culture.*

This is very similar to the first geography ability, but it approaches the question of
the relationship between geography and culture from a different direction. To use
brainstorming to practice this skill, and also simply as a technique to develop a set
of ideas students might start with on their projects, John first had them brainstorm a
list of geographical features, including climates, landforms, bodies of water, etc.
Then John selected one and asked students to brainstorm ways such a geographical
feature might influence the general pattern or major features of the way a culture
developed.

If students get in a rut of coming up with the same kinds of ideas — for
example, all transportation ideas — you might remind them of the need for
flexibility, originality, and elaboration. One way of doing this is to phrase the
question in this form: "Try to think of many, different, and unusual ways that …
[a range of mountains in the middle of a continent might influence cultural or
historical development on that continent]." You might also need to remind them to
look for global, rather than very specific, ways that the development of a culture
could be influenced by geography. You can do this without rejecting their very
specific ideas by asking how a given impact could have wider influence. For
example, a student might suggest that "Having many mountain ranges might make
building roads difficult." Asked what wider impact that might have, a student
might suggest that "This would make transportation difficult, which might result in
the virtual isolation of groups for extended periods of time, which in turn might
lead to the development of many different traditions within the same general
cultural group."

*Using brainstorming to think of ways that a culture might adapt different
geographic elements to its purposes*

The last skill in this set is different in that it emphasizes the fact that a culture is not
totally at the mercy of its geography, but can in fact make use of different
geographic elements to achieve its goals (rather than have its goals determined by
its geography). There are many ways you might use brainstorming to help students
think about this. What John did was have them brainstorm important features of a
culture they knew well — their own — first. They came up with things like
individualism, free enterprise, mobility, religious freedom, and many more. Then
he picked one and asked them to brainstorm ways that different geographic
elements might be used to support that feature of a culture. For example, using the
idea of individualism: large prairies could by used by a culture that valued
individualism as a way of letting each person have a great deal of personal space;
mountains could help individualists keep themselves apart from other people; in a
place that had many rivers, ease of transportation would allow individualists the
freedom to go where they wanted and to escape from society when they needed to;

a desert climate would lead to a sparse population, allowing people to be more individualistic; and so on.

This is a rather difficult idea, but it gives an example of how divergent thinking can support such complex thinking. Not all brainstorming will be like a storm in the sense of a rapid flow of ideas (although increasing the *rate* of that flow is a goal of practicing brainstorming). We hope this geography example has also shown how brainstorming can be both a technique for developing divergent thinking skills and a way to generate ideas for immediate use.

Those of you whose primary interest is in a kind of creativity very different from writing poetry, graphic design, or teaching geography, take heart: The examples we use below when introducing idea-generating techniques other than brainstorming come from different domains. We also have a list of ideas for brainstorming practice at the end of the chapter that will help you get started. But we hope you can already see how you can apply this technique — using brainstorming to improve divergent thinking skill — in other domains.

You should keep in mind that we've been using brainstorming here not primarily as it was originally intended — as a way to produce creative ideas — but rather as a form of mental exercise. We have a wide variety of "divergent thinking muscles," and our goal in using divergent thinking as an exercise, when there's no particular problem to solve, is to strengthen the particular divergent thinking muscles that matter to us. (In the case of the three examples above, we have been exercising our poetry-writing divergent thinking muscles, our graphic arts divergent thinking muscles, and our geography divergent thinking muscles.) Or, instead of focusing on improving just one set of divergent thinking muscles, you may wish to use a shotgun approach and exercise a wide variety of divergent thinking muscles to become a more all-around creative thinker.

### Beyond brainstorming

There are several other commonly used idea-generation techniques, most of which bear some similarity to brainstorming. Like brainstorming, they can help you when you're actually trying to solve a problem, write a poem, design a new widget, or invent a new dessert. They can also be used for mental exercise to build up specific divergent thinking skills.

### Forced associations

"Forced associations" is a technique to try when brainstorming isn't working. Sometimes it seems we get stuck — fixated — on a certain solution or a certain kind of idea, and as much as we try to think flexibly, all our ideas seem stuck in the same rut. To get out of such a rut, it's often helpful to force ourselves to give strange, outlandish, and patently hopeless ideas a chance. It often takes at least a dozen truly bad ideas to get one good idea, and we can't always short-circuit the process and go right to the good idea.

Here's how forced associations works. You need some kind of statement of the problem (e.g., "How can we get Janice to show more interest in schoolwork?"). Then you need a common noun, like "elephant." The dictionary is full of nouns that you might use, and it doesn't really matter which one you choose. In fact, if you pick something that doesn't work, or you find you don't like it, it's okay to change nouns at any time.

The trick is to come up with solutions — any solution at all — that in some way involves an elephant (or whatever noun you're working with). For example, we might have the elephant sit on Janice until she does her homework, or we might paint cheerful "School is fun" kinds of messages on the elephant and give it to Janice as a pet, or we might have the elephant shoot water at Janice when she says anything negative about school, or we might promise Janice a ride on an elephant as a reward for good work at school, or we might have the elephant sit on Janice's stereo so she can't listen to it when she should be doing schoolwork, or we might have Janice gather information about elephants and plan how to keep a small herd of elephants at school as mascots, or …

Think of your own dilemma, and try one of these nouns:

Cabbage

Thumb

Bookcase

Hammock

Puppet

Feathers

### *Getting out of mental ruts*

The point is, it's sometimes easier to break free from the mental straight jackets we often put on ourselves when we make the problem even harder by forcing an association. Our minds realize that realistic solutions are virtually impossible, which sets us free to be unrealistically imaginative. This sometimes yields an unexpected insight into the nature of a problem; it may result in a fresh approach that makes solving the problem more likely; or it may even produce a workable solution.

Forced association is also fun, like brainstorming, when used only as a cognitive callisthenic. If you're working with students who get tired of using the same brainstorming format (albeit with different content each time), it's a fun change of pace. The strange nature of the exercise also carries an intrinsic message that these activities should be fun, even silly, and not conforming. There can hardly be a "right" or "best" answer if you have to include an aardvark, or a cell phone, or a coloring book in every proposed solution to a problem.

### *Practice using forced associations*

Let's try a few examples to see how forced associations can be used as an exercise to develop a particular divergent thinking skill. Let's use as examples the problems of coming up with a topic for a science fair project and designing a science experiment.

Students who have been involved with science fairs, either as participants or observers, often get stuck in a rut, doing the same kinds of projects they and others have done before. To help them get unstuck, one might ask them to brainstorm (using regular brainstorming rules) science fair projects, with the condition that every idea must include a telephone, or a deer, or a dictionary, or a flower vase. (If science fair projects are a real problem you're working on, you might have them do all these exercises, on different days.)

### *Making it fun*

It's important to make it fun and to encourage a degree of silliness. It's also helpful if students understand the purpose of the exercise. Let them know that you don't expect that any of the actual projects they do will include telephones, rabbits, dictionaries, or flower vases. This is just a way to get their creative juices running. But keep a list, just as in any brainstorming activity, of all ideas. Seeing the list helps hitchhikers come up with new ideas, it encourages students to make an effort to come up with interesting ideas, and sometimes there will be an idea on the list that, with a few modifications, can be a genuinely useful and feasible idea.

As students get accustomed to this strange kind of exercise, they may get into a different kind of rut, such as including a telephone in every proposal by starting each idea with "I could call my friend on the telephone and tell her my idea, which is to ...." There are many roundabout (and often very imaginative) ways of avoiding the difficult but important rule of forced associations without actually breaking the rule. Keep flexibility and originality in mind. Encouraging ideas that are different than other ideas already suggested (flexibility), ideas that few people would think of (originality), or ideas that involve many interesting details that flesh out the idea (elaboration) will help students avoid circumventing the goal of "forced associations."

"Forced associations" can be applied to designing a science experiment, and it can be used both to solve a "real" design problem (e.g., one that a student might actually carry out) or as an exercise to improve one's divergent thinking as a scientist. It's important in either case to remember the goal of the activity, which is embodied in the rules of brainstorming. Don't set students up by pretending to be brainstorming, then being too quick to judge their ideas based on some standard you have of what would actually work. Judgment comes later, after the group has quit generating ideas either by regular brainstorming or by brainstorming with forced associations.

## *Staying on task*

Students may sometimes have trouble keeping on track — being allowed to get silly can be very seductive — and you may have to bring them back to the problem at hand from time to time.  One way to do this is to interrupt brainstorming possible solutions to a problem and directing the group to brainstorm the kinds of *criteria* they might use later to judge the ideas. We'll talk more about this technique in greater detail in the chapter on Creative Problem Solving, but we wanted to let know you know we're aware of this problem.  Allowing — even encouraging — students to be silly, to think in imaginative and divergent ways, can sometimes be a bit of a tightrope walk, with an ever-present danger of falling into nonproductive absurdity.  Just as there are ways to loosen up students' thinking when they're stuck in a rut, there are ways to keep it focused even when the goal is to avoid the obvious and to think of the unusual.  And as students become accustomed to doing divergent thinking exercises, either with the goal of solving a specific problem or as creative thinking calisthenics, they will learn to regulate the silliness level themselves.

## *Po*

Another interesting idea-generating technique was invented by Edward de Bono and is called "Po."  Its purpose is a bit different than a typical brainstorming situation.  Po can be a useful tool when one just wants play with ideas, to explore possibilities, or to break out of conceptual ruts.  We doubt that Po will ever be used much in everyday problem solving, but it can be a fun change of pace — and it's an excellent way to practice divergent thinking.

Here's how it works.  You start with a whimsical statement or a totally unrealistic wish, such as:

- Schools should have no walls, no grades, and no rules.

- Football should be played on a square field with four teams trying to take the ball in four directions.

- Cars should be able to control stoplights.

- Factories should all be downstream and downwind of themselves.

- Alarm clocks should be outlawed.

Then you respond to the whimsical statement in as many different ways as you can, trying to think of anything that might be interesting or helpful in the idea. Each response is an idea that somehow relates to the original idea — although there's no need to explain, or even understand, the connection. The original Po statement serves simply a stimulus to the imagination, as do any of the ideas that follow. Basic brainstorming rules apply, so there's no judging of ideas as you go.

### *What Po looks like*

Here's an example:

Po, Schools should have no walls, no grades, and no rules.

You wouldn't need vice principals, because nobody would be breaking school rules.

Schools should spend more time worrying about learning and less time worrying about rules.

Teachers could cooperate easily.

Students could study whatever interested them.

Students should be given more choices in school to empower them to control their own learning.

No one could be on the honor roll.

No one would *not* be on the honor roll.

Students would learn to learn, not to get grades.

Students might never want to leave school.

If there's a "no-rule" rule, then there's a rule.

Rules would work better if students designed them.

Students would have to evaluate their own learning.

Students and teachers would have to invent ways to cooperate.

Teachers would have to make classes really interesting to get anyone to pay attention.

Students would need to be independent learners.

Students would learn more because they'd spend all their time in classes that they like.

Students could learn at their own rate.

Classes should have more learning centers for students to work at independently.

### There's no goal with Po

It's important to remember that there's no particular goal here other than trying to quicken the flow of ideas. Adults tend to have more trouble with Po than children, who often engage in this kind of thinking quite spontaneously (and then are told all the reasons why their ideas don't make sense by well-meaning adults). We all know that schools without any rules at all won't work (perhaps you've read *Lord of the Flies*?); we know that chaos, not self-directed learning, would be the likely result. Perhaps there are good, workable ideas that could come from this kind of wishful-thinking kind of brainstorming; perhaps not. The point is, it doesn't matter whether something comes of it. In fact, if there's a goal to the brainstorming, such as coming up with new methods of school organizations, then it may be brainstorming, but it isn't really "Po." Po is not for solving problems. It's only for stimulating and stretching the imagination, for exercising our divergent thinking "muscles" in different ways.

### Plus-Minus-Interesting

"Plus-Minus-Interesting" is another idea-generating technique — a very useful one, with many obvious real-world applications — that can be used both to practice divergent thinking and to help us make difficult choices. Unlike traditional brainstorming, which is typically used when you have an idea what the problem is but don't have ideas how to solve it, or "Po," which is most often done *before* you define a problem, Plus-Minus-Interesting is most often employed *after* we have both defined the problem and come up with some possible solutions. Its goal is to help us decide which of the possible solutions we have devised will work best — with the possibility, of course, of improving on those solutions along the way.

Plus-Minus-Interesting was also developed by de Bono, who calls it simply "PMI," but as you will see, it's not such an unusual technique as Po. In fact, you may have used it already in solving problems or making choices — at least the "Plus-Minus" part.

Plus-Minus-Interesting employs divergent thinking, but in an important sense its goal is not divergent thinking at all, but rather evaluative thinking. With "Plus-Minus-Interesting," we start with three columns, such as the one shown. If you're working alone, you might simply do this on a blank sheet of paper turned sideways, but with a group it's best to start with a large sheet of newsprint for each heading.

*Table 1 (PMI)*

## PLUS-MINUS-INTERESTING

| Plus | Minus | Interesting |
|------|-------|-------------|
|      |       |             |

The Plus-Minus-Interesting process is rather like brainstorming in that some of the same guidelines about deferring judgment, avoiding ownership of ideas, and hitchhiking apply. The main difference between Plus-Minus-Interesting and brainstorming is the kinds of ideas you're trying to generate. With Plus-Minus-Interesting, you are looking for ideas that will help you evaluate an idea — possibly an idea that was generated by brainstorming.

*Putting Plus-Minus-Interesting to work*

In "Plus-Minus-Interesting," you start with a possible choice, solution to a problem, decision, or idea that you want to evaluate. Let's say you're thinking about taking an eighth-grade U.S. history class on an overnight field trip to Williamsburg (or, depending on where you live, you might imagine some site closer to home). What you do with Plus-Minus-Interesting is simply to list, somewhere on the chart, every idea you come up with in response to thinking about the field trip. Work with each idea, each response, that you come up with. Is it a plus, something that you think will be a benefit to your students or to you? Is it a minus, some kind of problem or reason you might not want to make the trip? Or is neither a plus nor a minus, just something that *might be* important or interesting (or might not be), simply something that came to mind that seems interesting but isn't necessarily either a reason to decide yes or no?

You may be protesting that the act of deciding under which heading to list an idea involves judgment, and didn't we say that the deferring judgment guideline was in effect? If so, you'd be right: You *do* need to think about the impact, to evaluate it as positive or negative, and this means judgment. But there's another kind of judging, or evaluating, that you should try to avoid at this stage. The kind of judging you are to defer until later is whether the idea or response that you came up with belongs on your list at all, or how important it is. What you don't want to do is to censor ideas at this stage or limit yourself to only the most persuasive arguments pro and con. If you do that, you may miss some very important ideas. The kind of judgment you are deferring is judgment about the quality of the ideas you are generating — even though the ideas themselves are evaluative ideas, ideas whose goal is to help you make a judgment about some other idea. Keep in mind that even though your goal in Plus-Minus-Interesting is evaluation, you are using divergent thinking as a first step in that evaluative thinking process.

Consider these three "minuses" that we might list for the field trip plan:

It would be very expensive.

Students would miss two days of school.

You'd have to fill out a form in the office, which is a nuisance.

All of these are things that might come to mind as possible minuses. They aren't all equal, certainly, and filling out the form really isn't much of a problem — not something that we'd give any weight to at all in making a decision about such a trip. But it came to mind, so rather than decide "on the fly" whether it's an important idea or not, we simply put it on the list, knowing that later we can weigh the various ideas as part of making a final decision. Probably we'll simply discard it later on — unless its presence on the list leads us to think of something else later on, such as:

I could have students fill out all the forms, make the reservations, plan the schedule, write a budget, etc.

This idea — an offshoot of an initial minor reluctance to fill out forms — we would probably list in the interesting column, or possibly under the plusses (if we thought the experience would be good for students).

There's no particular order to this: You don't hold off the minuses until you finish the plusses, or censor a plus because you're in the middle of the interestings. Nor are the three headings mutually exclusive. For the field trip listings, one might put "I'd see different aspects of 13-year-old behavior than I see in my classroom" under all three headings!

### *What's "interesting" about Plus-Minus-Interesting*

The "interesting" column deserves a few more words of explanation. In some ways it's simply a grab bag for ideas that don't fit anywhere else, but it's more than that. It's a reminder that some responses to an idea can be interesting, even important, without necessarily favoring or opposing the idea. In fact, having the column tends to encourage a wider range of responses than just having plus and minus columns. And often ideas that start in the interesting column grow, change, mature, and find their ways to one of the other columns — but if there had been no interesting column they might have been long forgotten.

### *Plus-Minus-Interesting for fun and profit*

Plus-Minus-Interesting is useful as part of actual problem solving, and as such we'll be looking at it again later on when we look at Creative Problem Solving (in Chapter 4). For now we just want to consider how it can be useful in exercising one's divergent thinking muscles — and how we can have fun with Plus-Minus-Interesting.

One easy source of Plus-Minus-Interesting targets is whatever emerges from doing "Po." For example, one idea from our Po list above suggested that there could be no more honor roll if there were no rules in a school. Another idea from that list suggested that students would have to evaluate their own learning. Either of these ideas — getting rid of the honor roll, or having students evaluate their own learning — might form the basis for an interesting PMI exercise.

Another source of Plus-Minus-Interesting targets is everyday life, in or out of the classroom. Whether our ideas have been developed in "formal" brainstorming/ brainwriting exercises or simply as the result of thinking about something, we have ideas — possible plans for action, decisions we might want to make, flashes of whimsy, or whatever — that are worth evaluating.

You can use almost any proposal. For example, in a U.S. history class we might propose — and have students evaluate using the Plus-Minus-Interesting technique — such ideas as:

- Pledging the flag at the beginning of each class (or getting the school to stop have the flag pledge every morning)

- Having group tests or other group-based assignments

- Adding a "balanced budget" amendment to the Constitution

- Having students evaluate the effects of some event or decision (Boston Tea Party, Emancipation Proclamation, Jay Treaty, the Puritans getting blown off course, the Federal system of government, etc.)

- Having students react to a hypothetical event that *might* have occurred in history, but didn't

Outside of class, real-life examples are abundant, such as:

- Schedule and lifestyle changes (What would it be like if we ate supper earlier or later? If we vacationed in the winter rather than the summer? If we got rid of our television? If we volunteered at the library? If we tried out for a play?)

- House arrangements and decorating (What would it be like if you and your sister swapped bedrooms? If we had a first-floor apartment instead of a third-floor apartment? If we painted this room pink? If we turned the dining room into a study and ate in the kitchen? If we put all the junk in the basement in storage and got a Ping-Pong table?)

Practicing Plus-Minus-Interesting with examples like these will help improve divergent thinking skill and, in many cases, may also result in some other direct benefit (such as learning more about the Jay Treaty or improving how you use the space in your house). As you choose topics to practice Plus-Minus-Interesting (for yourself, or for your students) remember what we know about task specificity. Unless there's a particular kind of creativity that you want to nurture, use a wide variety of examples focusing on different topics. That way you'll be likely to exercise and strengthen a wide range of task-specific divergent thinking skills.

Our last classroom exercise is one developed by our friend, David K. Hecht. He's a professor at Bowdoin College who has taught writing at many places, and he's contributed the following essay on an activity that has worked well for him:

Underlying          Patterns          and          Meanings          (UMP)

One activity, which can help identify both patterns and non-obvious meanings to words and ideas, can double as a kind of game.

The idea is this. Name three different objects or ideas that seem completely disparate. The "game" is to find a pattern that links the objects in an unexpected way.

Students should generate both the ideas (at the beginning of the exercise) and the possible solutions (at the end.) One recent running of the game came up with the following three items:

Olive,                              Necklace,                              Snowman

What you hope to encourage here is non-obvious responses. All three things are round (or at least have some round parts.) But that isn't really "out-of-the-box" thinking. Another possible pattern is that all three are "Common objects that only have very specific uses." Olives are found in a limited range of foods, necklaces can only be used to adorn one's neck, and snowmen are only found in sitting in yards.

Three even more disparate objects (from a later running of the same game) were:

Willy Wonka, Iron, Orchestra

Clearly, there is no obvious link between a fictional candy magnate, a personal item, and a group of musicians. For maximum effect, you should help ensure this disparity. If the first person calls out "Willy Wonka" and the second person "Baskin Robbins," you can ask for a different second item. A candy maker and an ice cream maker are a bit too close to make the game fun or rewarding.

Even with very disparate objects, there are still unexpected patterns. Here, for example, one link could be "Things which need to be managed carefully." Just as surely as hot iron must be tiptoed around, so too must one take care around the eccentric and temperamental Willy Wonka, and any organization with a lot of people — such as an orchestra — requires careful management.

Other examples from one running of this game:

EXAMPLE:                *Jogging,*                *Shampoo,*                *Lips.*
PATTERN: Fashion — things that people are concerned with to look better.

EXAMPLE:                *Lobster,*                *Sun,*                *Knife*
PATTERN:   Things   which   can   be   either   harmful   or   beneficial.

EXAMPLE:          *Chandelier,*          *Rodeo,*          *Shower*          *Curtain*
PATTERN:       Things       which       create       or       conceal       spectacle.

EXAMPLE:          *Astronaut,*       *Tea*       *Kettle,*       *Stop*       *Sign*
PATTERN:       Things       involved       in       rapid       motion       changes.

EXAMPLE:   *Séance,*       *Apartment*       *Building,*       *Sewer*       *System*
PATTERN: Things which facilitate connections.

It is not important that the patterns be definitive. Certainly, the idea of "connections" is not the only important thing about a séance, apartment building or sewer system. The important thing is that students get practice thinking of unexpected meanings or potential meanings of words.

I first used this exercise while teaching a writing course, specifically in a lesson on thesis design. It is very common for students to write thesis statements that list the points they want to make. One student, writing on United States culture after World War II, wanted to write a paper about suburbs, corporate greed, and McCarthyism.

Thesis statements like this tend to be clear, but they lack direction. Also, they are very limited. The basic point can be proven, but no fundamental underlying question can be analyzed. If, however, the student can see an underlying pattern with the elements of the thesis, that thesis can then become more ambitious. In this case, the student eventually realized that each thing was, in some way, about capitalism. The paper was then transformed into a deep analysis of how capitalist ideals helped create American culture.

I can see applications of this general method in a number of different disciplines — English, history, anthropology, economics. Any discipline that requires students to be able to look at new information in ways that might not immediately appear obvious could benefit.

— David K. Hecht

## *What to do when your thinking just won't diverge*

It's common that after brainstorming (or brainwriting) for a while, people get stuck. Either they can't think of anything else, or it feels like they're spinning their wheels, coming up with (basically) the same ideas again and again. Does that mean there are no more ideas?

No — there are always more ideas — but it may be time to quit. When brainstorming, most groups (and most individuals) will hit a plateau after a while. If they can deal with the frustration of mucking around and getting nowhere for a few minutes, there will often be a spurt of new ideas, and it's good to know that the lag in ideas is only temporary. Doing a "forced association" brainstorm — which actually makes the problem *more* difficult — often helps free the flow of ideas. But you don't want to make divergent thinking too much of a chore, especially when you aren't actually trying to solve a problem but only building divergent thinking skill for use later.

## *Incubation*

When a group (or an individual) runs out of ideas, often the best thing to do is simply to put the problem aside. There are many wonderful stories about geniuses (and other people like you and us) who had great insights after a period of "incubation." Incubation is like putting something on a cognitive back burner to warm and stew on its own for a while. Sometimes, after not thinking about something for an hour, a day, or even a week or longer, suddenly (and seemingly out of nowhere) new and sometimes wonderful ideas explode — just when we *weren't* thinking about them. You may have had this experience yourself.

Some people make very conscious use of this kind of unconscious, unattended thinking. For example, Nikola Tesla, the inventor of the AC generator, claimed that he created very detailed images of machines in his mind and then turned them on and let them run. He would let them continue to run in the back of his mind, unobserved, for long periods of time, periodically checking on them for signs of wear. This helped him design better machines without going to the trouble of actually building every prototype.

Psychologists disagree about the role of insight and unconscious thinking in creativity, but however it happens, something that *feels like* sudden insight does occur. And we can nurture that something if we're aware of it. We may not get as good at controlling our unconscious thinking as Nikola Tesla, but we can increase the likelihood of those "Aha!" experiences.

### Improving incubation skills

One way to do this is to tell our minds what things we want them to think about while we're doing other things. We can say things to ourselves like: "I just don't have the time, or the patience, to struggle with this right now. But I don't want to forget about it. I want some other parts of my mind to work on it, and to buzz me when they think they may have an idea."

Magic? Maybe. Will it work? Sometimes. Can we get better at this? Certainly — if we're willing to practice. So when you, or your students, run dry doing a brainstorming exercise, you might tell yourselves that you want to return to the same topic later. Just tell your unconscious mind to continue brainstorming, while your conscious mind tends to other things. And if you do this from time to time, you'll find that more and more often interesting ideas will just pop into your mind — as if by magic.

(John once heard this technique of putting aside a problem to let it incubate referred to as the "power of positive procrastination." Perhaps this is a helpful description, because it gently reminds us of the danger of putting a problem aside *too* long. At some point we must be sure to go back to it or our procrastination may not be so positive.)

### Movies that could help inspire brainstorming

There are wide arrays of movies about creative people doing creative things that may motivate creative brainstorming in the classroom. Some of these movies may not be appropriate for young children; other movies may have some objectionable content. You may want to consider taping these movies off of a network broadcast to get a "clean" version. Or you may enjoy watching them on your own time to arouse your own creativity!

*Shakespeare in Love.* As we mentioned before, this movie portrays one of the ultimate creative people, William Shakespeare, at his peak and writing *Romeo and Juliet.* The film shows the great playwright struggling with writer's block, falling in love, and creating a masterwork. *Shakespeare in Love* is particularly witty and insightful about showing how the creative process sops up one's everyday life for details and inspiration.

*Amadeus.* Like *Shakespeare in Love*, this movie won the Academy Award for Best Picture. *Amadeus* shows the interplay between creative genius (Mozart) and the merely good (Salieri). In addition to showing Mozart's own creative process, the movie may also spur discussion of the risk of creativity (such as professional jealousies).

*Dead Poet's Society.* This movie shows the impact a great teacher can have on a class. Robin Williams plays an English teacher who dares his students to explore their imaginations and challenge themselves.

*October Sky.* Unlike most movies about the creative process, *October Sky* focuses on scientific creativity. Homer Hickam, the son of a coal miner, joins forces with his friends to try to build rockets. A terrific exploration of how science can inspire, motivate, and stir the imagination.

Several other movies that may also work include *Finding Forrester, Mr. Holland's Opus, Off the Map, Frida, The Chorus, Vitus, Amélie,* and *All That Jazz* (which is more for adults).

### Some brainstorming topics

We promised earlier that we would end this chapter with a list of some topics for brainstorming practice. This is only meant as a "starter kit": Let your imagination roam freely as you devise your own brainstorming topics for yourself and your students.

- In what ways might one improve the rules of baseball (or other sport) to make it more exciting (or to make it more challenging, easy, interesting, fair, etc.)?

- In what ways might one use whole numbers and the processes of addition and subtraction to reach a total of 12?

- In what ways might one improve the design of automobiles (or ovens, houses, classrooms, schools, book bags, food containers, desks, computer keyboards, etc.) to make them more efficient (or to make them more user-friendly, environment-friendly, esthetically pleasing, inexpensive, etc.)?

- In what ways might one draw the same house (or profile, animal, tree, etc.) to show different aspects of it?

- In what ways might one use sound without words to communicate joy (or sorrow, fear, anger, love, etc.)?

- In what ways might one use a computer that most people would never think of?

- In what ways might one change a recipe to improve its taste, nutritional value, ease in preparation, etc.?

- In what ways might one determine the relative importance of different factors that influence the rate of growth of beans?

- In what ways might one write a word problem that applies the concept of adding, subtracting, multiplying, or dividing negative numbers (or that employs cube roots, perfect squares, multiplication as the inverse of division, division as repeated subtraction, etc.)?

- (When in the midst of reading a story): What things might the author do at this point in the story to solve the conflict?

- In what ways might one convince one's parents to buy an iguana for a household pet?

- What are some interesting things we might do right now?

- What are some topics about which it would be fun to brainstorm?

*Make your own list*

This would be a good time to start your own list of brainstorming topics, either for yourself or your class. And don't forget to push not only for fluency (lots of ideas) but also for flexibility (a wide range of ideas), originality (unusual, offbeat ideas), and elaboration (ideas with lots of details)!

CHAPTER 2

## BIBLIOGRAPHY

There are many sources of divergent thinking exercises (although the best source is your own imagination). One of John's favorites is Bob Eberle's *CPS for Kids*. Edward de Bono has published a number of books that teach interesting techniques like Po and PMI (and a wealth of other curious creative thinking skills).

As we noted at the end of Chapter 1, if you wish to pursue the idea of task-specific skills, you might try our recent edited book, *Creativity in Different Domains: Faces of the Muse* (Lawrence Erlbaum, 2005), John's book *Creativity and Divergent Thinking: A Task-Specific Approach* (Lawrence Erlbaum, 1993), or Howard Gardner's *Intelligence Reframed: Multiple Intelligences for the 21st Century* (Basic Books, 2000). Gardner's earlier book, *Frames of Mind: The Theory of Multiple Intelligences*, has had a major impact in education. His arguments for domain specificity in intelligence apply to creative thinking skills as well, and this book is worth reading even though divergent thinking skills are, in all likelihood, even more narrowly applicable than his seven (now eight) intelligences.

Finally, it's only fair to mention the inventor of brainstorming, Alex Osborn. Osborn worked on Madison Avenue and came up with brainstorming as a way to create better ideas for advertisements. His book, *Applied Imagination*, was first published in 1953 by Scribner's. The fine folks at the Creative Problem Solving Institute have published several articles and books that continue in this tradition.

CHAPTER 3

# MOTIVATION

## TWO "CREATIVITY TIME" CARTOONS

Some years ago John saw two cartoons about how *not* to teach for creativity. In one, a student is daydreaming some delightful and very creative things in the middle of a lesson. The student's thinking is related to the topic of the lesson, but it is clearly not the kind of thinking that is likely to produce a correct answer to the teacher's question. The teacher interrupts to remind the student that "Creativity Time" is not for another hour.

In the other cartoon, it is now "Creativity Time" in the same classroom. The teacher is giving very explicit instructions regarding the exact kind of project students are to create with the yarn, glue, and construction paper she is distributing — instructions that will make it difficult for anyone to produce anything very imaginative or unusual.

It was clear that this teacher didn't know much about creativity. And yet, she was doing *something* right, as we will see. As we hope to convince you in this chapter, it's very important to know what your goals are for a given lesson regarding creativity. Sometimes what we want is to encourage creativity in the work students are doing right now. Other times that's not what we want at all. Instead, what we want is for students to learn the "right" answer (for example, we don't want them to produce "creative" math facts; saying that 5 times 5 is 36 isn't creative, it's simply wrong). Or we want them to learn some skill, even at the expense of limiting their creative options in the activity at hand.

Motivation has a big impact on creativity, as we will see. The motivational constraints we set up in our classrooms will influence students' creativity in many ways. Knowing what our goals are for a given activity can help us decide if we should arrange things in ways that will promote creativity, or in ways that will favor some other kind of thinking. And we need to keep in mind that to encourage creativity in the long-term, we sometimes must sacrifice creativity in the short-term. But to do this, we first need to understand what kinds of teaching are likely to encourage, and what kinds are likely to discourage, creativity.

### Some questions about creativity in the classroom

Let's start with a few questions about the conditions for creativity — the motivational conditions — to focus the discussion. These questions are not a test of your creativity, and they don't have clear right-or-wrong answers, so don't worry too much about getting them right. We want to pose them before teaching you some things we know about motivation and creativity, and you may refer back to them as you work your way through this chapter to see if you can apply what you're reading to these situations. At the end of the chapter we'll discuss these situations, and what creativity research has to say about them, in some detail.

Each of the following five situations is followed by one or two questions. Take a moment to try to answer each question in the space provided. The goal is not to see if you can find the "right" answer, but rather to get you thinking about real-world situations in which we will be able to apply the motivation and creativity research results we'll tell you about later in the chapter.

*Situation 1*: Two groups of college students write poems as part of a psychology experiment. Assignment to groups is made at random. In one group, the students are offered $10 for writing the poems. In the other group, the students receive no reward.

- Which group do you think will enjoy the task more (by their verbal self-report)?

- Which group do you think will write more creative poems (as judged later by experts in the field)?

*Situation 2*: Two groups of elementary school children in their regular classes write science fiction stories. In one group, the students receive positive, but fair, evaluations, of their stories. In the other group there is no evaluation. The next day they write another science fiction story.

- Considering only the second story written by each student, which group will write more creative stories (as judged later by other teachers who do not know these students)?

*Situation 3*: Several groups of students make collages in art class. Some of the students express interest in the task, with others say they have little or no interest in making collages.

- Will there be a difference in the creativity of the collages made by those who express interest in the task and those who do not? If you predict a difference, which group do you predict will make more creative collages?

*Situation 4*:  Teachers A and B both require their students to do science fair projects. Mr. A asks students to "do a good job for me — make me proud!" and suggests that their performance at the science fair matters to him very much. Ms. B simply assigns the project.

- Which students will try harder (by their verbal self-report) to do good projects?

- Which students' science fair projects will be more creative (as judged independently by experts in the field)?

*Situation 5*:  In Classroom X, writing poems earns extra credit.  In classroom Y, the teacher gives no extra credit for writing poems, but tells her students "I know how much you like writing poetry, and I'd love to read your poems."

- Which teacher gets more poems to read?

- Which teacher gets poems that are more creative?

We hope these questions have piqued your interest about what is to follow. As we warned, many of these questions do not have simple answers that are clearly right or wrong. By the time you have finished this chapter, however, you will understand the issues involved in answering these questions and know under what circumstances one answer or another would be correct. More importantly, you will understand how the motivational constraints your students (and you) work under affect your creativity and how to manipulate the reward structure of your classroom to achieve your goals.

### *A little background about the "hidden costs" of rewards*

We all know that people will do things for rewards. Rewards motivate people to do things they wouldn't otherwise do (or to do more frequently things they would otherwise do less often). Employers, teachers, and parents routinely use this knowledge to influence the behavior of others, both in planned, conscious ways (e.g., gold stars and bonus paychecks) and in unconscious, automatic ways (e.g., smiles and nods of approval). The giving and receiving of rewards is a regular part of human interaction.

What many people don't know is that rewards can also make behaviors <u>less</u> likely to occur — they can actually *decrease* the frequency of the desired and rewarded behavior — under certain conditions. Let's give an example.

### *A typical "hidden cost of reward" research study*

Most preschool children enjoy drawing. Given the opportunity, drawing is one of many activities preschool children will spontaneously choose to do.

In one preschool, it was observed that during time when children could choose their own activities, they spent, on average, about 16% of their time drawing. Rewards were then offered for drawing during this free-choice period. Children were still free to choose whatever activity they wanted to do, but if they chose drawing, they would earn a reward (a certificate with a gold seal and ribbon).

Did the amount of time spent drawing increase? It certainly did — preschool children love rewards, just like the rest of us, and they were happy to spend more time drawing in order to receive them.

So where's the problem? It came later, after the reward for drawing was taken away. Now conditions were just like before the reward was introduced: Drawing was one of several activities children could choose, with no inducement offered for picking any particular activity.

When researchers observed the children in the preschool a week or two later, they found the students now chose drawing only about 8% of the time — far less than the 16% rate before rewards had been briefly introduced (and subsequently discontinued). In a matched control group observed during the same period of time, the average amount of time spent drawing did not changed throughout the entire time the study was being conducted.

### Learning what is fun and what is work

What does this mean? It's as if (and we need to emphasize the *as if*) the children were saying to themselves something like this: "Gee, I got paid for drawing! I thought drawing was something people did just for fun, but now I can see it's actually work, because people get paid for *working*, not for playing and having fun. I liked the reward, of course, so I was happy to do a little work drawing to earn the reward, but now that there's no reward, I don't want to spend my time working. I'd rather do something fun!"

Preschoolers don't actually think thoughts like that, of course (they tend to use more split infinitives). But something happened in the study we just described that changed the interest of a group of preschoolers in drawing. Similar studies with older children and adults confirm that this is a common phenomenon.

### Intrinsic and extrinsic motivation

It appears that, while rewards do increase how often people perform rewarded behaviors, rewards also tend to undermine the *intrinsic* interest of a task. *Extrinsic* motivation — doing things for rewards (such as grades or money) or because other people want us to do them — tends to undermine *intrinsic* motivation (doing things because we like to do them). This is a common finding, although it's often forgotten in our rush to reward children for doing anything we like. Perhaps that's one reason why students gradually find reading less and less intrinsically rewarding as they progress through school. Most (although not all) primary-age students enjoy reading, but this interest tends to decrease as children get older (and as they receive rewards for reading, and as they hear the message that reading is work, which schools unintentionally convey).

It is interesting to note that this same principle is used in dog training. For example, although some people like it when their dogs bark, most people don't. Yet dogs like to bark (particularly James's new puppy, Kirby). Counter intuitively, one of the best ways to get Kirby to stop barking is to give him a treat whenever he barks. He'll come to associate barking as a rewarded behavior — like sitting and staying — and then won't want to offer it for free!

But dog training or students' interest in reading isn't what this chapter is about. We tell you about this "hidden cost of reward" because of its relationship to the subject of this chapter: motivation and creativity. Intrinsic motivation, it turns out, is a key to creativity. Now you probably aren't surprised to hear that people are more creative when they do things because they find them interesting than when they do the same things for rewards. When James was interviewed on Spanish television and the last question was asking for a take-home message about creativity, his mind went blank and all he could think of was, "Love what you do." He later kicked himself because it sounded so trite. Yet it's also so true.

It may be a little more surprising to learn that offering rewards tends not only to increase extrinsic motivation (that's the point of rewards, after all), but also to *undermine* intrinsic motivation. And since intrinsic motivation is associated with creativity, decreasing the level of intrinsic motivation (by increasing the level of extrinsic motivation) does, in fact, decrease creativity.

That's the key idea of what is to follow, although as you will see, that single idea has many interesting ramifications. In the next section we'll restate the intrinsic motivation hypothesis and describe a few studies that have been conducted to test what it can tell us about creative performance. Then we'll come back to some practical applications of this research.

## *The intrinsic motivation theory of creativity*

Although many people have done work relating to motivation and creativity, the research conducted by Teresa Amabile and her colleagues has been the most influential in this area in recent years. The five studies that we will describe below are all the work of Amabile.

We've already stated the basic idea behind the intrinsic motivation theory of creativity: People are more creative when the reason they do something is its intrinsic interest (as opposed to doing something because someone else wants it done). Doing things for rewards, or any other kind of extrinsic motivation, results in decreased creativity. To help you understand how complicated this simple concept can become — and the importance of some of those complications — we're going to tell you about some experimental results and flesh out the theory based on the situations described in those experiments. We believe this kind of bottom-up approach will be easier to understand, and to apply to new situations, than a top-down, theory-based explanation.

There are two things to keep in mind in all of these studies. First is the importance of the motivations people *perceive* as being most important in a given situation. We may enjoy doing something, such as woodworking, and under most conditions we would do that activity just for fun. But if we are offered a reward for doing it, or if we believe that our work is going to be evaluated in some way that we think is important, then that increases our extrinsic motivation. And when extrinsic motivation increases, intrinsic motivation naturally decreases. (If you doubt that increasing extrinsic motivation almost always has the effect of decreasing intrinsic motivation, read on. We believe the results of these five experiments will convince you.)

The other thing to remember is that Amabile is looking at creative *performance*, not creative thinking or creative motivation. Creative performance is something that can be observed and even measured in ways that creative thinking or creative motivation cannot. What Amabile (and others) have done is to have participants write poems, tell stories, make collages, and do other tasks that result in some tangible product. These products are then given to groups of experts to be evaluated for creativity. For example, poems are evaluated by poets, poetry critics, and poetry teachers; collages are evaluated by artists, art critics, and art teachers; and so on, with a different group of experts for each kind of creative product. Although each judge works alone and doesn't know anyone else's judgments of the creativity of these products, there is a remarkable degree of agreement about which poems, stories, collages, etc. are the most and the least creative.

### Five experimental studies about motivation and creativity

Okay, let's look at five representative experiments. Amabile and her colleagues have actually conducted dozens of studies to probe the effects of intrinsic and extrinsic motivation under different conditions, but these five studies will provide a good sense of the implications of the whole range of studies. Although for our purposes we will label them "Study 1, "Study 2," etc., these experiments were not actually done in the order that we will present them.

*A word of warning*: This is the one section of the book that looks at creativity research studies in some detail. The discussion may seem a bit technical at first, but we believe that learning about some of this research is the most effective way to understand how to apply in the classroom what we now know about intrinsic and extrinsic motivation. Take your time and try to understand each of the five studies, but don't let yourself get too bogged down in details. If the studies don't make complete sense the first time through, continue on to the section on *Application of the Intrinsic Motivation Theory of Creativity*. After reading how these research results can be applied in classroom situations, the studies themselves may make more sense — and as long as you understand the applications, you don't need to master every detail of the research studies themselves.

*Study 1.* In this study, 72 creative writers (most of who had published either poems or stories, with the remainder being students who had completed at least one creative writing course) wrote poems that were judged by experts for creativity. First Amabile had each subject write a haiku on a "Snow" theme. Then subjects read a short story for 15 minutes. Finally, they wrote another haiku poem, this time on the theme "Laughter."

Before writing the second poem, Amabile had two-thirds of the subjects do one other thing. (The remaining third made up the control group.) The experimental group subjects spent five minutes rating the importance of seven reasons why they liked writing. There were two lists: One listed seven reasons for writing poetry that all reflected intrinsic motivation (e.g., "enjoying the opportunity for self-expression" and "liking to play with words"), while the other list included only reasons related to extrinsic motivation (e.g., "enjoying or hoping for public recognition" or "having been encouraged by teachers or parents to go into writing").

Amabile wasn't actually interested in the particular rank orderings of the reasons for writing poetry that the two groups of subjects made. What she wanted to do was to make very salient either intrinsic motivation or extrinsic motivation. That is, she wanted to induce one group to focus on intrinsic motivation, and the other group to focus on extrinsic motivation (while the third group, the control group, was not encouraged in either direction).

On the first poems ("Snow"), there was no difference in the average creativity ratings of the poems. The three groups all had mean creativity ratings of approximately 18.4 (on a 40-point scale). These poems were written before Amabile had them do anything else, and the equal creativity ratings among the three groups can therefore be taken as evidence that the three groups had equal skill in writing creative poetry.

On the second ("Laughter") poems, however, there were significant differences among the three groups. The control group had a mean of about 18.9 (on the same 40-point scale); the intrinsic group was about one point higher; and the extrinsic group had a mean rating more than three points lower than the control group (and four points lower than the intrinsic group).

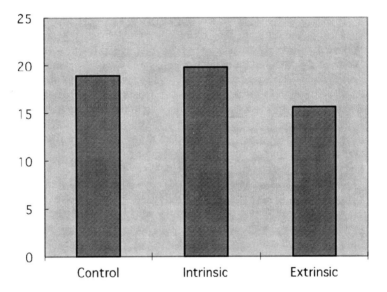

*Study 1. Mean creativity of poems.*

This study represents, first of all, a rather straightforward confirmation of the intrinsic motivation theory of creativity, and we started with this particular study because it is in many ways the simplest of the five we will tell you about. But we think it is significant for another reason. Amabile was dealing with adult creative writers, all of whom reported spending many hours each week writing and to whom writing was clearly a very important activity. And yet with a simple five-minute activity — rank ordering a list of reasons for writing — she managed to have a very significant impact on their levels of creativity. If talented, dedicated adult writers can be so readily influenced in their motivations (and levels of creativity), is it unreasonable to expect that children can also be influenced by a bit of verbal magic (like "reminding" them of the interesting aspects of the tasks they are doing)?

There is one other important point to be made about this first study. Did you notice that the decrease in creativity when extrinsic motivation was highlighted (in comparison with the control group) was much larger than the increase in creativity under conditions favoring intrinsic motivation? To some extent this is typical: It is generally easier to increase extrinsic motivation (and decrease creativity) than it is to increase intrinsic motivation (and increase creativity). But this was also a very special group — all people who devoted significant amounts of time to creative writing, but none of whom had (yet) become rich or famous from their writing — in which it is likely that initial levels of intrinsic motivation were already fairly high. For this reason, increasing their levels of intrinsic motivation was probably a more difficult task than increasing their levels of extrinsic motivation. This may account, in part, for the much larger differences between the extrinsic group and the control group than between the intrinsic group and the control group.

*Study 2.* This study looked at the effects on creativity of two things that are related to extrinsic motivation: the expectation of evaluation, and having an audience while working. Subjects made collages, using a set of about 100 pre-cut shapes, a large poster board, and a bottle of glue.

There were two differences in the instructions the subjects received. First, half of the subjects were told that a group of artists was waiting to evaluate the collages the subjects were making and would give the subjects feedback about the quality of their work. Evaluation was not mentioned to the other half of the subjects. These two conditions were called "expecting evaluation" and "not expecting evaluation."

Both of these two groups were further divided into two subgroups, making four different conditions in all. Subjects in two of the subgroups were told that they were being observed through a one-way mirror (the "audience" condition), while for the other two subgroups a curtain was drawn across the glass (the "no audience" condition). Thus there were four conditions: Expecting evaluation-Audience; Expecting evaluation-No audience; Not expecting evaluation-Audience; and Not expecting evaluation-No audience.

All subjects worked alone in a room. As for the age of the subjects, Amabile actually conducted two nearly identical studies like the one we're describing, one involving elementary school children, and another with college students. The results were very similar, so the results appear not to be dependent on age.

After subjects had completed their collages, the collages were all evaluated by artist-judges, who worked independently of one another and did not know which collages came from which group of subjects. Here are the results:

Expecting evaluation-Audience          17.2

Expecting evaluation-No audience       19.1

Not expecting evaluation-Audience          20.6

Not expecting evaluation-No audience       24.0

Both factors which were expected to increase extrinsic motivation did in fact lower creativity, both when they occurred separately (the Expecting evaluation-No audience and Not expecting evaluation-Audience groups) and when they occurred together (the Expecting evaluation-Audience group).  The effect appears to be cumulative, as the Expecting evaluation-Audience group was significantly lower than either of the conditions in which only one of the factors was operative (as in the Expecting evaluation-No audience and Not expecting evaluation-Audience groups).  And when neither kind of extrinsic constraint was in place, creativity was at its highest.

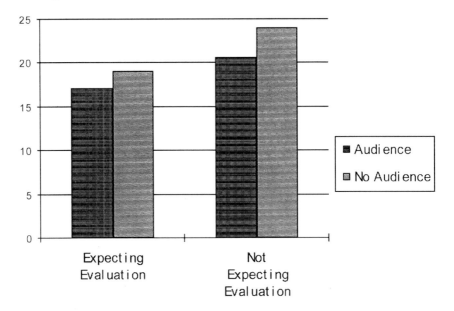

*Study 2. Mean creativity of collages.*

So expecting to have one's work evaluated and having an audience when working both appear to decrease creativity significantly.  Does this mean that having *any* kind of audience — even people who just happen to be in the same room — will decrease creativity?  That's the question that the next study tried to answer.

*Study 3*. This study was similar to Study 2, in that there were actually four groups, with half of each group expecting evaluation and the other half not.  This time there was no one-way mirror, however.  This time half of each group worked alone, while the other half worked in a room with three other people who were also subjects in the experiment.

This time the subjects were all college students, and the task of interest was writing a poem. Subjects were told that the study was about handwriting, however, not about creativity or poetry. The experimenters explained that, in order to get a useful sample of a person's handwriting, it was necessary for them to write something original. If one simply copied something or wrote something from memory, the researchers had learned, it tended to distort the writer's handwriting somewhat and handwriting samples obtained that way did not reveal as true a picture of one's personality. The subjects in this handwriting study were therefore all being asked to write a short poem — a haiku. That way, the explanation went, the handwriting analysts would have similar, but original, samples of each subject's handwriting.

We've already told you that half the subjects worked alone and half worked in a room with three others. All subjects worked individually, however, to produce their own poems. And half of each group was told that, as part of the study, the poems would be evaluated, while the other half was told that the content of the poems was unimportant.

There were therefore once again four groups: Expecting evaluation-Audience; Expecting evaluation-No audience; Not expecting evaluation-Audience; and Not expecting evaluation-No audience. The differences between this study and Study 2 are in the nature of the audience. This "audience" could not actually see the work the subjects were doing, because unlike collage-making, which is very easy to observe from a short distance, it is hard to actually see what someone else is writing. The audience could see that the participants were indeed *writing*, but not the actual words they were writing or the poems they were creating. For this reason, the subjects were aware that it was impossible for the audience to evaluate their poems or make judgments about how they went about their work. The audience in this study could also be seen (rather than observing through a one-way mirror, as in Study 2), and the audience was not a separate group of people but other participants, and thus perhaps more like peers than teachers.

The results were similar to those of Study 2 in regard to the effect of expecting evaluation. The subjects in the two "expecting evaluation" groups wrote much less creative poems than those in the two groups that were not expecting evaluation. But there was no adverse affect of this audience — which was not really so much an audience but simply other people who happened to be nearby. The "audience" and "no audience" groups wrote equally creative poems.

It is clear that expecting evaluation decreases creativity. It also seems that some kinds of audiences decrease creativity, specifically audiences that are in a position to judge one's work, while other audiences who cannot observe the actual work one is doing do not have a negative impact on creativity.

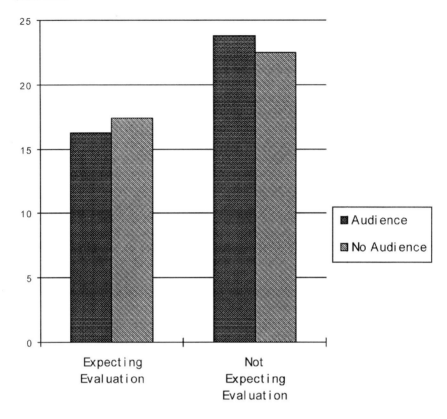

*Study 3. Mean creativity of poems.*

*Study 4.* The subjects for this study were elementary school students in grades two through six. Each student worked alone to create two artworks, one a "spin-art" project (in which subjects created a design by sprinkling dots of colored ink on a card before it was spun on a turntable), the other a collage. For the control group, there was no evaluation of either project. These students were told that the experimenter was a student teacher who needed practice working with students doing art projects.

For the experimental group participants, the first project was evaluated twice, once midway through and again at the end. The idea was to create an expectancy of evaluation in the second, collage-making project, and also to examine the effects of two different kinds of evaluation, task-based and person-based. Task-based evaluation involved giving positive feedback focused on aspects of the work itself (such as "These colors work nicely together to give a warm feeling"). Person-based evaluation involved giving positive feedback focused on the skill of the child (such as "Your work shows that you have a good sense of color").

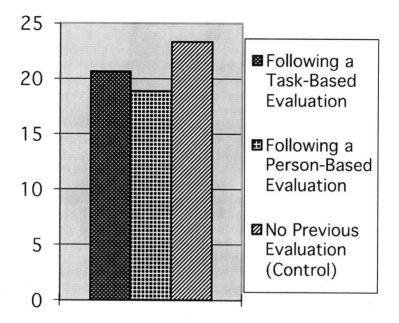

*Study 4. Mean creativity of collages by type of evaluation.*

What Amabile found was that any expectation of evaluation — an expectation based in this case simply on the fact that the previous work had been evaluated — tended to decrease creativity. Task-based evaluations were not so bad as person-based evaluations, however.

There was one other part to this experiment. In each of the two experimental groups (the task-based evaluation and person-based evaluation groups), half of the subjects were simply told that the "student teacher" needed practice working on art projects with students. The other half were also told that, if the students did good work, it might help the "student teacher" get a job at another school.

Adding this additional instruction, which makes the evaluation of the collage of greater importance, further decreased creativity. That is, the students who received this additional information suggesting that the quality of their work might affect the student teacher's chances of getting a job produced less creative collages, whether they were in the task-based evaluation or person-based evaluation group.

It appears that evaluation has a generally detrimental short-term impact on creativity, although if the evaluation focuses on the task rather than the person that effect is somewhat minimized. Furthermore, increasing the importance placed on the evaluation tends to increase the detrimental impact on creative performance (that is, the more important the evaluation is perceived to be, the lower the creativity of one's work).

*Study 5.* The subjects in this study were all undergraduate women who were recruited from an introductory psychology class to participate in an experiment on person perception. This person perception experiment required a videotape player, which shortly after the session began broke down. The videotape player had, in fact, been rigged to do just that. Subjects were then informed that they would not be able to continue with the person perception experiment, but they were recruited instead to take part in a different study the experimenter was doing. This other experiment involved making a collage.

Subjects were induced to take part in the collage-making experiment in four different ways. One group was simply told that since they couldn't complete the person perception study, in order to receive their introductory psychology experimental participation credit they would need to do the other, collage-making study. This is the No choice-No reward group.

A second group was given a choice. They were told they had met their obligation and would receive their introductory psychology experimental participation credit for the person perception study, but as they were already there and had the time, would they mind taking part in the collage-making study? This is the Choice-No reward group.

The other two groups were told that, unlike the person perception study (for which subjects received experimental participation credit only), in the collage-making study subjects were being paid $2.00. Subjects would still get their introductory psychology experimental participation credit, but would also receive the $2.00 for the collage-making study. Subjects either had a choice whether or not to participate (Choice-Reward group) or were simply told that they would do the collage-making task rather than the person perception one (No choice-Reward).

The reason the fake experiment was used was to enable Amabile to make it clear that, for the subjects who received a reward and had a choice, they would see themselves as participating in order to receive the reward, while a similar group would do the same task without reward (and without knowing that any other group received a reward, of course). By the way, no one declined to participate, which was quite fortunate. Otherwise it might have led us to question the outcome, whatever it might have been.

The results were intriguing:

| | | |
|---|---|---|
| No choice-Reward | 315 | (Highest possible score = 560) |
| No choice-No reward | 270 | |
| Choice-No reward | 260 | |
| Choice-Reward | 225 | |

The highest creativity was achieved by those who in the No choice-Reward group, and the lowest creativity scores went to the Choice-Reward group. It appears that there is what psychologists call an interaction effect, in which the two variables do just that — interact — to produce an outcome not predictable by looking at either variable in isolation.

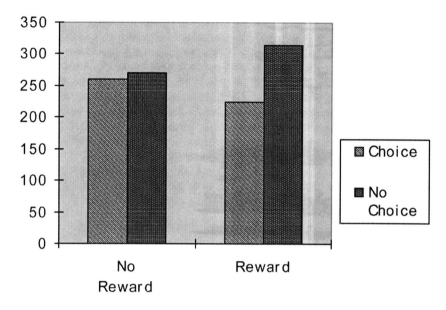

*Study 5. Mean creativity of collages.*

How can we explain these results? The low creativity of the Choice-Reward group makes sense, for this group had the strongest reason to think that their motivation was extrinsic — that is, they were doing the task for the reward. The $2.00 reward, although not a large sum of money, was very salient. These subjects were likely to perceive the situation as one in which they were asked to make the collage in return for a payment of $2.00. Thus, for them, their understanding of why they were making the collage was likely to emphasize extrinsic motivation — doing it in order to receive the reward.

In the two groups that received no reward, there was nothing in the experimental design that suggested either intrinsic or extrinsic motivation. The experimenter did not emphasize either in any way. The motivation of these subjects was therefore most likely somewhat mixed, depending primarily on how much they liked making collages.

But what about the highly creative No choice-Reward group? Shouldn't the $2.00 "reward" have pushed them in the direction of extrinsic motivation and therefore had a negative impact on their creativity? The answer is no, but the reasoning is a bit complicated. Remember that these subjects had *no choice* whether or not to participate, so they were not likely to see themselves as participating in order to earn the $2.00. Instead of functioning as a reward (and making extrinsic motivation more salient), the $2.00 was more like a pleasant surprise, a sort of bonus which they would receive, but *not* as a condition for making the collage. They were therefore unlikely to think of the $2.00 as a reward; it was simply an aspect of the situation that made the situation more pleasant, and it perhaps therefore made the collage-making more enjoyable. This may have given them more of a sense that "I'm doing this because I enjoy it" than would have been the case in any of the other groups, whose motivations may have been more like "I'm doing this only because I have to" (as in the No choice-No reward group), "I'm doing this as a favor to the experimenter" (as in the Choice-No reward group), or "I'm doing this in order to earn $2.00" (as in the Choice-Reward group). That is, the $2.00 received by subjects in the No Choice-Reward group would not be likely to increase extrinsic motivation, but instead have the effect of raising intrinsic motivation because it simply made the task seem more enjoyable.

Okay, those are some of the basic research findings. Let's use the situations that were described at the beginning of the chapter to see how to apply these ideas.

*Application of the intrinsic motivation theory of creativity*

Re-read each situation and try to answer the questions that follow it, basing your answers on the research you just read about. Then read our discussion of each situation.

*Situation 1*: Two groups of college students write poems as part of a psychology experiment. Assignment to groups is made at random. In one group, the students are offered $10 for writing the poems. In the other group, the students receive no reward.

- Which group do you think will enjoy the task more (by their verbal self-report)?

- Which group do you think will write poems judged as more creative by experts in the field)?

*Discussion of Situation 1*

Based on the "hidden cost of reward" research, we should predict that the group that received no reward would like the activity more. There's actually quite a bit of research in the area of psychology often called "cognitive dissonance theory" — an area that is intimately related to the "hidden cost of reward" studies — that tells us that people will indeed report less interest in an activity that they have been paid to do.

As far as the creativity of the poems, Amabile's work leads us to predict that the same group (the one that received no reward) will write more creative poems.

### *What if writing the poems was required, not optional?*

There are a few "Yes, but ..." qualifications to be made here, however. First, one might ask, "What if the task was *required*, and the $10 was not a reward?" (as in Study 5 above). That would change everything, of course, and it is an important point. Only if the students thought they were writing the poems *in order to receive the reward* would the $10 function as a reward (and have a negative impact on their creativity). If they thought they had to write a poem anyway, then the $10 wouldn't be a reward but rather just something that made the situation more pleasant. In that case, the group that received $10 (but not as a reward) would be expected to write more creative, rather than less creative, poems.

There is one more "Yes, but ..." qualification to consider, but let's stop for a moment and think about applications of the first one. If a teacher wants her students to do something — let's say, for example, that she wants them to write poems — and she wants to encourage them to be creative, should she offer a reward (such as extra credit)? No, she shouldn't — at least, she shouldn't offer the extra credit *as a reward.* She might require all students to write poems and at the same time do something to make the situation pleasant (such as play music the students liked), but the "reward" should not be offered or perceived by the students as a reward, and receiving it should not be contingent upon writing the poetry. Giving students extra credit in this situation without lowering creativity would be difficult, we think, because no matter how you present it to them, students are likely to think of the extra credit as contingent on writing a poem, even though the poem-writing task is a required one. But that doesn't mean that the teacher can't do everything possible to make the situation a pleasant one — and she might bear in mind what we learned from Study 1. Just reminding students of the interesting aspects of writing poetry is likely to boost their creativity.

### *Why students' initial level of intrinsic motivation matters*

The second "Yes, but ..." qualification we want to make has to do with students' initial level of interest in writing poetry. Many students enjoy writing poetry, and many others that don't will do so simply because it's a required activity. But if what you want is to get students to write *many* poems — for example, if you want them to build skill in writing a particular kind of poem — and if the students are unlikely to write poems unless they are rewarded, then rewards may be justified. (At $10 per poem, we suspect you could collect a rather large sample of students' poetry very quickly!) Rewards and other extrinsic motivators may lower intrinsic motivation and reduce creativity in the short term, but the practice and skill-building may be worth it in order to reach other, long-term goals. As we'll see in many of the situations that follow, extrinsic motivation also has its place, even in the development of some of the skills needed to be creative in the future.

A final "Yes, but ..." qualification is sort of obvious, but nonetheless important. If the teacher told some students that they would receive $10 and told other students that they would receive nothing, and if the students receiving nothing knew that other students were getting $10 for their poems, this would change everything. The No reward students, apart from whatever protests of unfairness they might make, would also be likely *not* to have high levels of intrinsic motivation under this scenario.

Why is this important? Typically in any class, students' initial levels of intrinsic motivation are very different. A teacher might know that *some* students would not write poems without some kind of reward, and if she wanted them to write poems in order to build some skill, she might decide to reward those students and at the same time prefer *not* to reward some other students, whose intrinsic interest in writing poetry was higher. Unfortunately, in many cases she won't be able to have it both ways, and she may sometimes need to decide which goals — increasing the skills of students who are low in intrinsic motivation, or protecting the levels of interest and creativity of students who have more intrinsic motivation for that particular task — are more important at that particular time.

*Situation 2*: Two groups of elementary school children in their regular classes write science fiction stories. In one group, the students receive positive, but fair, evaluations, of their stories. In the other group there is no evaluation. The next day they write another science fiction story.

- Considering only the second story written by each student, which group will write stories judged as more creative by other teachers who do not know these students?

### Discussion of Situation 2

This is rather straightforward. According to the research we looked at, the students who received evaluations will write less creative stories on their next outing. The reason for this is that they are more likely to expect evaluation, having just received an evaluation of their earlier story. And we know that expectation of evaluation increases extrinsic motivation and decreases creativity.

There is an important "Yes, but ..." for this situation also, similar to a qualification introduced in the discussion of Situation 1 but perhaps of even greater importance. This time it's evaluation, not reward, that is pushing extrinsic motivation to the forefront and lessening creativity. Evaluation — giving students feedback on their work — is a key aspect of good teaching. Is there any way to evaluate without decreasing intrinsic motivation?

### To evaluate, or not to evaluate, that is the question

Unfortunately, the answer is for the most part no — most evaluation tends to cause people to focus on extrinsic motivation, on getting it "right," on meeting others' expectations — but that doesn't mean the situation is hopeless. Although in the short term, evaluations of their writing will decrease the creativity of students' writing, the long-term consequences are more complex. While having *every* piece of writing evaluated is likely to have a very negative long-term impact on one's intrinsic interest in writing and on the creativity of one's writing, evaluation is also feedback, the kind one may need to improve one's skills. If a student is interested in writing science fiction, she will nonetheless need to learn about character development, plotting, even sentence structure and spelling, and to learn these things she will need feedback from someone who can teach her these things.

But must all feedback be viewed as evaluation? Probably not, and there are certainly ways to lessen the negative impact of such feedback. First, not every piece of writing should be subject to evaluation. Let some writing be just for fun, even if doing the writing is required. Second, task-based evaluation has less of a negative impact than person-based evaluation. Third, the importance of the evaluation *as an evaluation* (in terms of how it will affect a student's grade, the respect that she can expect in the future from the teacher, etc.) should be minimized. What should be emphasized instead is the *information content* of the feedback, and how the student can use that information to shape her work in the future.

### *Keeping your goals in mind*

And finally, we must remember that we can't do everything. Sometimes the goal of increasing skill by providing feedback is simply more important than the short-term impact on creativity. For some things, such as spelling or math facts, we really are not interested in creativity anyway. And for many others, such as writing, drawing, or solving mathematical word problems, we care both about getting it "right" in terms of meeting certain standards of performance and also in producing interesting, creative work. In those cases, we need to decide what is our goal at that moment, for that particular activity, and set up the task constraints (in terms or rewards, evaluations, etc.) accordingly. This is what the teacher in the cartoons we discussed at the beginning of the chapter got right (despite everything else she was doing wrong) — and why it's so important that we keep in mind what our goals are for each lesson vis-à-vis creativity.

*Situation 3*: Several groups of students make collages in art class. Some of the students express interest in the task, while others say they have little or no interest in making collages.

- Will there be a difference in the creativity of the collages made by those who express interest in the task and those who do not? If you predict a difference, which group do you predict will make more creative collages?

### *Discussion of Situation 3*

Unlike the other four situations, this one is exactly what you would expect, even without any knowledge of the work of Amabile. Her basic idea — that people tend to be more creative when they do things they enjoy than when they do things they don't enjoy — seems like just common sense when applied in a simple situation like this one. There's not even a "Yes, but ..." worth mentioning here. We included this situation among the five because we wanted at least one situation that was fairly transparent — just to remind you that not every teaching situation is terribly complicated!

*Situation 4:* Teachers A and B both require their students to do science fair projects. Mr. A asks students to "do a good job for me — make me proud!" and suggests that their performance at the science fair matters to him very much. Ms. B simply assigns the project.

- Which students will try harder (by their verbal self-report) to do good projects?
- Which students will produce science fair projects judged to be more creative by experts in the field?

## *Discussion of Situation 4*

There's nothing in the research we've told you about that will help you answer the first question, but the common sense answer is correct. Students will work hard to try to please their teachers, and Mr. A has made it clear that he will be pleased if his students work hard on this project, so they will.

The second question is more difficult. Amabile's research (especially Study 4 above) suggests that when students do something to please someone else, that is extrinsic motivation and it leads to lower creativity. So other things being equal, the students in Ms. B's class will do more creative science fair projects.

Now here comes the "Yes, but ...." If the students in both classes are interested or otherwise dedicated enough to do the project without further encouragement, then yes, Ms. B's class should produce the more creative projects, as their motivation will be less extrinsic and more intrinsic than that of Mr. A's students. (Remember that increasing extrinsic motivation always comes at the expense of lessening intrinsic motivation.)

## *The judicious use of extrinsic motivation*

But for such a long-term activity as a science fair project, intrinsic motivation may flag at times. And for some students, there may be little intrinsic motivation at all to create, conduct, and analyze the results of a science experiment.

For students who would otherwise make only a token effort (or less) on a time-intensive activity like a science fair project, a large dose of extrinsic motivation may be needed in order to get them to do anything at all. And to be creative, one must do something. (Woody Allen once said that "Ninety-five per cent of life is showing up." And Thomas Edison's "Genius is one percent inspiration and 99 percent perspiration" comes to mind when thinking of the importance of extrinsic motivation, even in the service of creativity, when one's intrinsic motivation just isn't enough to keep you going.) Unless students are motivated in some way — either extrinsically or intrinsically — they won't do anything at all. Intrinsic motivation is better, especially in terms of creativity. But if one lacks sufficient intrinsic motivation to motivate one to do the job, then extrinsic motivation may be necessary. So if having students do a science fair project is important — to learn about experimentation, say, or about some special topic, or for whatever other reason — then extrinsic motivation may be both helpful and even necessary to produce that outcome. And even in regard to creativity, if doing *nothing* is the alternative, then doing *something* — even if it is only to please someone else (or for some other reward) — is going to result in a more creative outcome.

We mentioned the possibility of students' intrinsic motivation flagging at times, even among students who have a fairly high level of initial interest in the activity. Very few things are interesting *all* the time, and most activities include both fun parts and parts that feel much more like work. For this reason, on a long-term project like a science fair experiment, a combination of intrinsic and extrinsic motivation may be ideal. That way, at times when it is hard to remember the intrinsic interest of the activity — and it happens to everyone, even doing things they love — the extrinsic motivation can help keep one plugging away. We'll discuss this more below in the section on helping students manage their own motivations.

*Situation 5*: In Classroom X, writing poems earns extra credit. In classroom Y, the teacher gives no extra credit for writing poems, but tells her students "I know how much you like writing poetry, and I'd love to read your poems."

- Which teacher gets more poems to read?

- Which teacher gets poems that are more creative?

### Discussion of Situation 5

We hope the pattern of answers to the questions and the "Yes, but ..." qualifications is becoming clear. Except for Situation 3, these are complex scenarios, but there are common features among the various complications.

First, the teacher in classroom X will definitely receive more poems. Students, like all of us, will do things for rewards. Depending on the value of the extra credit, Teacher X may be inundated by poems, regardless of the initial level of interest in writing poems among her students.

What about the creativity of the poems? Well, based on Amabile's work one is tempted to answer that the poems received by Teacher Y will be more creative. Teacher Y encourages intrinsic motivation (by saying "I know how much you like writing poetry, and I'd love to read your poems") and does nothing to promote extrinsic motivation, while Teacher X is emphasizing extrinsic motivation by offering a reward. What could be more clear-cut?

### *Quantity versus quality*

The trouble is, Teacher X will probably receive *many* more poems than Teacher Y. Even though the average creativity of Teacher X's poems may be lower than those of Teacher Y, if you simply look at the total number of highly creative poems received by each teacher, or if you compare the creativity of only the most creative poems received by each teacher, then the students of Teacher X will likely win. To some degree at least, quantity leads to quality.

So does that mean teachers should offer extra credit to students for writing poems? Not at all. It means that *sometimes* that might be the most appropriate choice.

### *Adjusting task constraints to match student needs*

With students who are already interested in writing poetry, Teacher X's offer of extra credit runs the risk of lowering intrinsic motivation, and for little gain. Students are already interested enough to write some poems, so what's the point of rewarding them just to increase the numbers of poems Teacher X gets to read? Probably the students will indeed write even more poems under reward conditions than they would without the reward, but unless the goal is to promote extensive practice writing poems, emphasizing quantity isn't a very sound idea when students are already interested enough to do a good bit of writing on their own. Especially when the increase in quantity is achieved at the expense of intrinsic motivation.

With students who otherwise wouldn't write poems, more of a case can be made for Teacher X's extra credit system. If Teacher X's goal is to help students gain a better understanding of a certain kind of poetry (e.g., by giving extra credit for sonnets only), then this kind of reward is certainly justifiable. Where there's little intrinsic motivation to start, offering rewards can't lower the level of intrinsic motivation much. And perhaps by providing some extrinsic motivation to get students started, some may be able to discover how much fun it is to write poetry (thereby having the long-term effect of increasing their intrinsic motivation).

### *The trick of requiring work, but promising not to evaluate it (and keeping your promise!)*

There's another way to manage this situation, however, that in many cases will be better than the approach of either Teacher X or Teacher Y. If you want students to write poems (or write stories, paint pictures, create math puzzles, etc.), then you can *require* that they do so — but at the same time promise *not* to evaluate (or reward) their efforts. Explain that each student *must* do whatever it is you want them to do, and that you will check to make sure they have done it (and hound them until they do), but that you will not grade or otherwise evaluate their work. Some students may do the minimum possible, of course, but if your goal is to encourage creativity, you need to accept the risk that some students will not accept that encouragement every time you offer it.

It's important to note that you can't go back on a promise not to evaluate students' work, because if you do, they won't believe you next time you make that promise. Even if some students abuse the situation, you must give them credit for doing the work if they did what you asked, however minimally. And remember in the future not to make such a promise at times you can't keep it.

### *"It depends": The need for professional judgment*

So the general answer to whether to reward or not to reward, to evaluate or not to evaluate, to encourage extrinsic motivation or not to encourage extrinsic motivation is often "It depends." As for intrinsic motivation, it's probably good to encourage it whenever you can, but that's not nearly so easy to do as to encourage extrinsic motivation. Sometimes the best we can do to enhance intrinsic motivation is simply to get out of its way and *not* undermine it by emphasizing extrinsic motivation.

There's no simple one-size-fits-all answer to the puzzle of how best to motivate students, but we believe that understanding the intrinsic motivation theory of creativity and how to apply it can help us make better decisions, on a case-by-case basis, regarding the use of rewards, evaluation, and other strategies that influence motivation. One thing *is* certain: If we are going to make wise decisions about when to encourage extrinsic or intrinsic motivation, we have to be clear about what our goals are. Do we want to encourage creativity in our students right now, in this particular activity? On the other hand, is what we want to do right now more along the lines of building skills for future use? Creativity is important, but so is skill development. There is room for both in the ways we structure our interactions with students, and we needn't apologize for sometimes, even often, choosing skill development over creativity as our primary objective for a given lesson. We need to plan for both, however: We need both to encourage creativity by enhancing intrinsic motivation and to encourage skill development (often by employing techniques that emphasize extrinsic motivation). And in doing both these things, we need to be clear about what our objectives are in the lessons that we teach. Finally, we need to keep in mind the overall picture: What long-term attitudes do we want students to develop? And what mixture of rewards, evaluations, and doing it just for fun will lead to those kinds of attitudes?

### HELPING STUDENTS LEARN TO MANAGE THEIR OWN MOTIVATIONS

*Sometimes extrinsic motivation is better than no motivation at all*

In the first chapter of this book we confessed that, even when doing things that we very much enjoy, like woodworking or writing, our interest in and energy for a task can occasionally desert us. Sometimes that means it's time to do something else for a while, but other times we really want to continue, but we know that we need some kind of motivational boost. That may involve reminding ourselves of why we enjoy the activity, why we think it's fun or interesting or personally rewarding. But trying to revive an ebbing intrinsic motivation doesn't always work. Another technique John uses to pump up his *extrinsic* motivation is by thinking of how much his daughter or wife will enjoy the results of his woodworking labors. Indeed, we both do this by bearing in mind the deadline that an editor has set for whatever writing we're doing (like this book!), or whatever other extrinsic motivator will work at the moment.

When we do this we know that increasing our extrinsic motivation will have a negative short-term impact on our creativity, but we are sometimes willing to accept a lower level of creativity when what we need at the moment is to get some work done, even if it isn't our most imaginative or original work. We know that *part* of any job, even a job that involves a great deal of creative thinking, is only routine work, work that needs to be done but which requires neither a great deal of creative thinking nor any intrinsic motivation. It just needs to be done.

*Boosting intrinsic motivation drives out unwanted extrinsic motivation*

On the other hand, we also sometimes find ourselves doing things for the "wrong" reasons. We realize that we are caught up in thinking about rewards, contemplating expected evaluations, or doing things simply to please others — that is, focusing on extrinsic motivations of one kind or another — at times when we know what we need to be doing is thinking creatively. Often that happens because something in our environment has reminded us of those various extrinsic constraints. Times like that, when we become aware that our reasons for doing what we're doing have gotten pushed too far away from the intrinsically motivating reasons for doing work that we enjoy, we can stop and remember why, at other times, we have found that work so interesting, so enjoyable, so exciting, so much fun.

*But not everything has intrinsic interest*

Let's be frank: We don't find all the work we do intrinsically interesting. We don't generally find grading tests, cleaning the house, or many other tasks that we routinely do interesting, enjoyable, exciting, or fun. Indeed, think of the first job you had, whether working at McDonalds, delivering papers, or mowing lawns. It was likely something that was not fun and that you would have never chosen to do. When we must do those kinds of tasks, the best we can do is try to reinforce the real, extrinsic motivation we have to complete the activity and get on with it. But if you let some activity that you usually enjoy turn into work, it's time to have a talk with yourself.

*Teaching motivation management as a metacognitive skill*

This kind of self-talk is something that we can do, and should do, for ourselves. It is also something we should teach our students how to do for themselves. But it's not something that a teacher can explain once and then forget about. Learning how to massage one's own motivations takes time. Explaining the need for such monitoring and adjusting of our motivations, teaching students how to do it, modeling this kind of behavior, and reminding students when it might be appropriate to engage in this kind of self regulation are all part of the process of helping students learn to manage their own motivations.

Teachers need to teach students when and how to use many other metacognitive skills, such as:

- how and when to adjust reading speed to suit one's reading objective

- how and when to estimate to check one's computations to make sure the results are making sense

- how to use study time effectively

- how to use different idea-generation heuristics, such as brainstorming and forced associations, at appropriate times (see Chapters 2 and 4!)

- how to monitor reading comprehension to make sure one is making sense of what one reads and not just reading the words

Learning when and how to monitor (and to take action to adjust) one's own motivations is, like all the strategies and techniques in the list above, an important metacognitive skill that we need to teach our students.

There is no special trick to teaching this skill. One should bear in mind that until they are in the upper grades of elementary school, most children have a great deal of difficulty applying metacognitive strategies on their own. Young children can learn to use such strategies, but they often need to be told each time it is appropriate to use them.

Older children can not only learn to use these self-talk strategies to manage their motivations, they can also understand why such management is helpful and, over time, learn to do such self regulation spontaneously. But they will learn this only if we take the time to explain the need for such self regulation, if we demonstrate when and how to use this kind of self-talk, and if we cue them at times when it might be appropriate (especially when we see that extrinsic motivation has pushed aside intrinsic motivation and they need to remind themselves of the interesting, personally enjoyable or rewarding aspects of the activities that they are forgetting at the moment).

## Managing classroom goal structures

As explained in the first part of this chapter, it is important to manage the goal structure of a classroom. Teachers should keep in mind their immediate and long-term goals, and with those goals in mind try to:

- encourage intrinsic motivation when the goal is to encourage creativity (or when one wants simply to build interest in some activity, which is important in its own right) by telling about, showing, and reminding students of the interesting and enjoyable aspects of whatever activity students will be doing.

- use extrinsic rewards sparingly, which generally speaking means only when needed to motivate students who otherwise would not engage in an activity that we believe they need to do, such as many skill-building activities.

## Individual motivational management by students

Equally important, however, is to teach students how to do for themselves what we as teachers are (or should be) doing for them. We need to teach them how to manage their own internal goal structures (how to massage their own motivations) in ways that will help them:

- be more creative and be more interested in the things they do, and also

- be able to remind themselves of rewards and other extrinsic motivators when necessary in order to complete tasks that they do not find intrinsically interesting

Teachers who do these two things will help their students become creative people who find a great deal of joy in the things they do. That's quite a gift to give anyone.

## BIBLIOGRAPHY

The best place to go for information about how motivation influences creativity is Teresa Amabile's *Creativity in Context* (Westview, 1996), which should be available in any college library. Before this, she has published *Growing Up Creative: Nurturing a Lifetime of Creativity* (Crown Publishers, 1989), which is less theoretical and has more practical suggestions for parents and teachers. She has also written numerous articles and chapters in edited books. Her former student Beth Hennessey summarized the field in Kaufman and Sternberg's *Cambridge Handbook of Creativity*. John has also published several research studies demonstrating that the negative impact of extrinsic constraints is especially severe among adolescent girls. He summarized this research in a paper he delivered at the American Psychological Foundation's 2005 meeting, which can be downloaded from his webpage, http://www.rider.edu/~baer/index.htm.

Alfie Kohn makes the general case against the use of extrinsic motivation very well in *Punished by Rewards* (Houghton Mifflin, 1993). We think he goes a bit far in his blanket indictment of rewards — we believe there are times when they *are* appropriate and bring about more good than the harm they cause — but his summary of the evidence is honest, fairly complete, and up-to-date. There is also a much older and somewhat more technical book of articles about (and titled) *The Hidden Cost of Rewards* (edited by Mark Lepper and David Greene and published by Erlbaum in 1978; available in most college libraries), which includes much of the early research in this area and remains a superb resource. And for a taste of the debate about whether to use rewards in classrooms, the February 1991 issue of *Educational Leadership* includes a series of four articles by Bob Slavin and Alfie Kohn in which the two authors argue back and forth about the potential good and harm of rewards when used as part of cooperative learning.

## CREATIVE PROBLEM SOLVING (CPS)

### A PUZZLE

Here are six steps in creative problem solving. Can you put them in order?

*Solution-Finding: Choosing a Solution*

*Idea-Finding: Generating Possible Solutions*

*Mess-Finding: Exploring a Situation*

*Data-Finding: Gathering Information*

*Action-Planning: Developing a Course of Action*

*Problem-Finding: Defining the Problem*

Take a moment — but not too long — to think about the order in which these steps might go.

Was this easy? Some parts of it probably seemed obvious. For example, it makes sense to choose a solution *after* you generate possible solutions, so however else you ordered these steps, you probably put Idea-Finding before Solution-Finding.

There's not a single "right" answer to this puzzle (which is one reason we told you not to spend too much time on it). Like so many things, the answer to how to order these steps is, in part, "It depends." We want to emphasize this at the outset, because although we will teach you a model of creative problem solving that puts these steps in a particular order, we want you to remember that, depending on the situation, it often makes sense to do things in different ways. As you practice this CPS model, we'll encourage you to take the steps in the order we're about to teach you. But after you're familiar with the model and each of its steps, you'll need to adjust what you do to fit the particular problem you're working on. When you use CPS to solve real problems, you have our permission to alter the order of the steps as you see fit. In fact, we insist upon it!

### *When to use CPS*

Before we teach you CPS, we need to explain when you might use it. The P — for "problem" — in CPS is a troublesome word, because when people think of problems, they usually think of negative things, unpleasant situations, things they'd rather avoid. There certainly are problems of that kind, but there are also other kinds of problems that few of us would want to avoid, such as deciding:

- how to spend a $10,000,000 lottery prize

- where to spend a month's vacation

- which of several job offers to accept

Many problems fall somewhere between things we'd want to avoid and the kinds of examples we just gave of "problems' we'd love to have. For example, trying to find a way to make your engine run smoother (if you have a mechanical bent) is a problem; how to get a certain color combination to work in a room (if interior design is more your thing) is a problem; and figuring out what to do for a science fair project (if that's something you, or one of your students, finds challenging) is a problem. Depending on your level of interest, these problems may be negative, positive, or neutral.

The point is that the word "problem," as used in CPS, doesn't refer to how much we like or dislike a particular situation. It refers to any situation that we might like to change or improve in some way. One of John's favorite slogans is:

Creative thinkers see opportunities where others see only problems.

This way of thinking about problems — as opportunities to make something better — is the way we'd like you to think about problems as you read through this chapter.

Given this broad definition of "problem," it would seem that almost anything would fit, and to an extent this is true. CPS can help guide one's creative thinking on almost any kind of project. It's most useful, however, for difficult problems that don't have a single right answer.

One other caution: CPS takes time. If you need the answer quickly, or if you simply don't care enough about the situation to spend much time thinking about it, then CPS probably isn't a good way to go. Or you may want to use it, but to limit the time you put in on some of the steps.

To give you an idea how ready you are to learn CPS, complete the *Are You Ready to Learn CPS?* checklist and follow the directions for scoring it.

### Are you ready to learn CPS?

This brief checklist is *not* a measure of what you know. It is simply a way to assess, for yourself, some attitudes that are important in learning CPS.

Respond to all the questions honestly, recording your answers to each question on the line before each question number. Use this scale:

4 = Definitely true

3 = Mostly true

2 = Only slightly true

1 = Definitely not true

___1. Do you believe it's possible for you to become a better problem solver?

___2. Do you believe it's important for you to become a good problem solver?

___3. Are you willing to spend time developing your problem-solving skills?

___4. Do you like to "play around" with ideas in your head?

___5. Are you willing to try out new ideas?

___6. Do you consider yourself to be open to new experiences and opportunities?

___7. Do you think being imaginative is important?

___8. Do you have a strong desire to improve yourself using CPS methods?

___9. Do you believe that being a better problem solver will help you at work, at school, or at home?

___10. Will you have the support and encouragement of others in your efforts to learn CPS?

Now total up the points you gave in answer to each question. Your total will be somewhere between 10 and 40.

If your score was 30 or more, you are definitely ready to start.

If your score was between 15 and 29, you may not be quite ready. Is there any chance that you could adjust your attitude about some of the questions to which you responded either 1 or 2?

If your score was below 15, it's probably not a good time to start learning CPS. But that's not likely, because if you don't think it's possible to become a better problem solver (Question 1), or you don't believe it's important to be come a better problem solver (Question 2), or you don't think it's worth the time it might take to become a better problem solver (Question 3), then it's unlikely that you would have read this far. You may also have seen some connections between questions on the *Are You Ready to Learn CPS?* checklist and some of the ideas we've been considering in Chapter 2 about divergent thinking and Chapter 3 about motivation (Questions 4, 5, 6, and 7).

## THE CPS MODEL

The CPS model is sometimes called the Osborn-Parnes model after Alex Osborn, who you learned in Chapter 2 was the inventor of brainstorming, and Sidney Parnes, who was a primary developer of this technique of creative problem solving.
Here are the six steps of the CPS model, in their correct order:

*Mess-Finding: Exploring a Situation*

*Data-Finding: Gathering Information*

*Problem-Finding: Defining the Problem*

*Idea-Finding: Generating Possible Solutions*

*Solution-Finding: Choosing a Solution*

*Action-Planning: Developing a Course of Action*

Let's explain what each step means, which will make the order of the steps make more sense.

### Mess-Finding

Mess-Finding means being open to experience, freely exploring opportunities, looking at old solutions in different ways, and thinking about things one might like to change (either because the current situation is somehow unpleasant, or because one senses that a tolerable or even pleasant situation could be improved). Mess-Finding is being attuned to ways one's life, or a particular situation one is dealing with, might possibly be made better. It doesn't focus on how to make things better, or even exactly what the better outcome would be. It is simply an awareness of a situation that one senses it might be worthwhile to work on. The end result of Mess-Finding is the acceptance of some challenge, some situation that one has decided to try to improve.

Some messes come to us not as the result of sensing an opportunity for improvement ourselves, but rather because someone else has sensed such an opportunity and has given us the challenge to do something about it. But it doesn't matter the source of the mess. What matters is that one:

- *recognizes* a situation that one believes could possibly be improved,

- *doesn't know how* to improve the situation, and

- is willing to *devote some time* to trying to find ways to make the situation better.

- *Data-Finding*

Data-Finding is gathering information about the situation. This includes the kinds of things we normally call facts (Who, What, When, Where and How kind of facts), and it also includes impressions, feelings, and other very subjective kinds of information. This is *not* a search for solutions, but it may involve considerable analysis of the situation. The goal of Data-Finding is to understand the current situation, including its problematic aspects, as thoroughly as possible.

### *Problem-Finding*

Problem finding is a very important step, and one that is frequently overlooked. Once people feel they understand the situation — that is, they conclude what we're calling Data-Finding — they tend to rush immediately into trying to find solutions. In doing so, they often end up missing what could have been much better solutions because they didn't take time to consider different ways to conceptualize the problem.

Here's a story, one that we've been told is true although we can't prove it. Because this story has been around for so many years, it has probably changed over time from the truth of the actual event. But it could be true (and we hope it is), and that's all that matters.

Here's the story: The owner of an office building in a major city had a problem. His building had only two elevators, and his tenants complained that these elevators were much too slow. Some were even threatening to move out.

The owner asked an elevator company what it would cost to speed up the elevators. They came up with a few possible solutions, ranging from retro-fitting the two old elevators to make them faster (for $1,000,000) to building two brand new elevators (for $4,000,000).

The owner didn't want to spend so much money, but he couldn't afford to lose his tenants. He was talking it over with a friend one day, and he wondered if there might be some other way to speed up the elevator service.

His friend suggested he think about the problem differently. "You're trying to solve the problem of how to make the elevator service faster. But the real problem is how to keep your tenants happy, and especially how to keep them from being upset by the elevators. Making the elevators go faster might solve the problem of how to keep them from being upset, but I think there might be a much easier way."

"What way is that?" the owner of the building asked.

"Why not just install large mirrors on all the landings where people wait for elevators? Then it won't *seem* like so long a wait, and they won't mind the time they spending waiting for the elevator."

It worked — in fact, it worked so well that it's hard these days to find an elevator where the landings aren't decked out in full-length mirrors. (We are such a vain species — and we also like to watch other people surreptitiously!) And it exemplifies a very important point about the importance of Problem-Finding: The way we think about a problem can have a major impact on the kinds of solutions we conceive.

We tend to find solutions that fit problems as we've defined those problems. And our definitions of problems often include limitations — often in the form of assumptions about what kinds of solutions we're looking for — that are not necessary, and that keep us from finding some of the most interesting solutions.

Here's another example. Imagine you are troubled by mice in your house. You have set mouse traps, but mice keep getting in.

You might think of the problem as "How might I build better mousetraps?" If you succeeded, that would be wonderful, but it's easy to see that you would be unnecessarily limiting your range of possible solutions by defining the problem so narrowly.

You might widen your definition to "How might I be more effective in catching mice?" Possible solutions would include better mousetraps, but also such things as cats, devices other than traps that catch mice, and poisons.

You could continue to widen the problem definition to something like "How might I avoid having mice in my house?" Possible solutions to this problem would include all the solutions listed above for catching mice, and it might also include things like finding and filling in the holes that give the mice access to your house and simply moving to another house or neighborhood. It might also include solutions that would try to steer the mice away from your house, such as cleaning up an area in your yard that seems to be a favorite nesting area (or hiring a Pied Piper?).

This is probably as broad a definition of the problem as we would use, but you could cast a still wider net. How about "How might I not be bothered by mice?"

This would include catching mice and avoiding having them in your house — that is, all the solutions listed above — but it would also allow such possibilities as ways to learn to get along with mice, finding ways to not notice them, etc. We're not big fans of mice (although James does have four pet rats) and we wouldn't care to change our opinion of having them around, so a problem definition this broad wouldn't be any better than the previous one (that is, "How might I avoid having mice in my house?"). But for someone with a more open mind regarding the possibilities of sharing their house with mice, "How might I not be bothered by mice?" could be a more productive way to state the problem.

The goal of Problem-Finding is to be as sure as you can that:

- you haven't limited yourself unnecessarily by the way you define the problem, and

- the problem you're working on is truly the problem you want to solve.

### Problem-Finding's magic words

So far we've been talking about not limited yourself unnecessarily, and we hope you're beginning to understand how to do that. (There will be lots of practice to come.) To help you make sure that you're working on the right problem, here are some magic words that will help:

"In what ways might I …?"

"How might I …?"

These magic words are the words you will use to begin *every* problem statement that you make. Either set of magic words is good as the other — they mean essentially the same thing — so just use whichever is more comfortable or natural for you. But it is essential that you use one of them, however silly it may seem at first! *Every* problem statement in CPS begins with either "How might I" (or "How might we" in the case of a group working on a problem) or "In what ways might I" (or "In what ways might we"). What follows these magic words depends on the nature of the mess you're working on.

What makes these words magic? It's their power to direct your problem-solving energies toward *solutions* rather than toward complaints or restatements of what bothers you about the situation. This way of framing a problem statement also pushes you toward solutions that focus on what you really <u>want</u>. These magic words will help you avoid doing what we often waste our problem-solving energies doing, which is focusing on what's wrong with a situation rather than how we might make it better. In the next section, when you will be using CPS to try to solve a real problem situation in your life, we'll ask you to use these magic words.

And we'll encourage you to use them any time you're working on a difficult problem.

## *Idea-Finding*

Once you've decided what problem you're going to try to solve (that is, you've decided which of your "How might I ...?" statements best fits your goals for the situation you want to improve), it's time for Idea-Finding. Idea-Finding means developing and listing a wide variety of possible solutions to the problem statement, then narrowing down the list to just a few. (As you will see below, this two-step process of generating lots of ideas — often by brainstorming — and then narrowing the list down to a few of the best ideas is actually part of each step in the process.)

Sometimes when you're working by yourself on a problem, somewhere along the way — and often during the Idea-Finding phase — you will come across an idea that immediately seems ideal to you. At that point you need to decide if the idea really is that good, in which case there's no need to look for or evaluate any more ideas, or if the idea just seems so good because you're tired or frustrated or simply anxious to find a solution, in which case you might do well to continue the process of Idea-Finding.

## *Solution-Finding*

When you're using CPS in a group to solve a group problem, sudden inspirations are less common, or at least it's less common for everyone in a group suddenly to agree on a solution. But whether you're working alone or in a group, at some point you need to shift your focus from brainstorming to the selection of the most promising ideas. There's no fixed number, but typically it's helpful to select a handful of the most interesting and promising ideas and move on to Solution-Finding.

In a sense, Solution-Finding is a continuation of the winnowing process begun in Idea-Finding. The goal is to find a way to evaluate the promising and interesting ideas that you came up with during Idea-Finding. The difference between Solution-Finding and the evaluative part of Idea-Finding is that in Solution-Finding, explicit criteria are developed to evaluate ideas. Then those criteria are applied, and an optimal solution is found.

The first part of Solution-Finding is brainstorming a variety of possible criteria. What standards might one use to judge candidate solutions? Some of these criteria will directly reflect elements in the problem statement, because if a solution doesn't solve the problem, it is clearly not a good solution. Other criteria of good candidate solutions include such things as cost, feasibility, time requirements, and ethical considerations.

After generating a list of possible criteria, you select the most important criteria and use these to evaluate the handful of ideas that were the end result of Idea-Finding. This evaluation will, you hope, lead you to a clear idea of how you want to solve the problem. Solution-Finding may also involve a great deal of refining, combining, and strengthening the candidate solutions to make them even better (now that you've generated a list of criteria and you're more clear about what an ideal solution would look like).

## Action-Planning

The final step is Action-Planning. This is another step that is too often neglected. Countless good ideas haven't work because:

- no one looked ahead to assess possible sources of assistance and resistance,

- no one developed a plan and a time table for implementing the solution, or

- no one thought about how to monitor progress along the way to determine how well the plan was working and what adjustments might be needed.

Action-Planning involves doing all these things. Sometimes Action-Planning results in new challenges — new messes — that also need a bit of CPS work. You may have what seems like a wonderful solution, but there's just this one problem .... That's great, but rather than ignore that one problem area and proceed hoping for the best, it's usually better to problem solve more on the difficult aspect of the solution you've chosen.

## Divergent thinking and evaluative thinking

Every step of CPS involves both a divergent thinking phase, in which you generate lots of different and imaginative ideas, and an evaluative thinking phase, when you refine and select ideas. Sidney Parnes once used one of those collapsible hat or towel racks, the kind made of several slats of wood that form a series of diamonds with a peg at each intersection, to explain to John the relationship between divergent thinking and evaluative thinking in CPS. You can push the sides of those hat/towel racks together to make the diamonds very narrow and tall, or pull the rack apart to make the diamonds very short and wide. It's the same in CPS, he said: First you diverge, opening yourself up to lots of ideas, and then, as part of the same step, you must evaluate those ideas and narrow them down to just a few.

**ALTERNATION BETWEEN**

# Imagination

And

# JUDGEMENT

## DIVERGENT THINKING AND EVALUATIVE THINKING

The "Alternation between Imagination and Judgment" graphic is an illustration of one of those divergent thinking/evaluative thinking diamonds. This two-part process makes up each step of CPS. First comes divergent thinking — getting lots of ideas by using one's imagination freely. This is followed by evaluative thinking — judging ideas, deciding which ones are the best, or perhaps the most workable, at a given point in time.

The wider one diverges at any stage of CPS, Sidney Parnes explained, the more one must converge. Some problem solving is easier — or sometimes you simply don't have much time — and so you produce fewer ideas in the divergent thinking stages. With fewer ideas to consider, less evaluative thinking is required, because there are fewer options to choose among. But the key idea is that at every step in the process there is an alternation between imagination and judgment — between divergent thinking and evaluative thinking.

### *Seeing the CPS process as a whole*

We've been looking at CPS, step by step, to learn how it works. Soon we will be using it, step by step, to solve a real problem. But it will be instructive to take a minute now to examine the illustration of "The CPS Model of Creative Problem Solving" to get an overview of the *entire* CPS process.

*The CPS model of creative problems solving*

**CPS
STAGE**

**DIVERGENT PHASE**                     **EVALUATIVE PHASE**

| DIVERGENT PHASE | CPS STAGE | EVALUATIVE PHASE |
|---|---|---|
| Opportunities are explored Situations are searched for possible messes | **MESS FINDING** | Challenge is accepted Systematic effort is taken to respond to challenge |
| Data are gathered Situation is examined from many viewpoints Info, impressions, feelings are collected | **DATA FINDING** | Most important data are identified and analyzed |

| Many possible problem statements are generated in the form "In what ways might I (we) …?" | **PROBLEM FINDING** | A working problem statement is chosen |
|---|---|---|
| Many different ways of responding to the problem statement are developed and listed | **IDEA FINDING** | Ideas that seem most promising or interesting are selected for further examination |
| Many possible criteria are formulated for use in reviewing and evaluating ideas | **SOLUTION FINDING** | The most important criteria are selected<br>These criteria are used to evaluate, refine, and strengthen ideas |
| Possible sources of assistance and implementation steps are identified | **ACTION PLANNING** | Specific plans are formulated<br>Roles are assigned<br>Timeline is set |

This illustration once again makes the point that there is a divergent thinking phase and an evaluative thinking phase to each step in the process. It also indicates some of the special issues that are likely to arise or be considered in each of these phases at different stages in the process.

It's important to note that the CPS process isn't static or rigid. By this we mean you don't always do it exactly as outlined. Although when you're learning CPS, it's wise to stick to the steps very closely, later you will adapt it to suit the specific problem you are working on and the particular constraints you are working under. Sometimes you will have a flash of insight early on and short-circuit some or all of the remaining steps. Other times you will find yourself going back to stages you thought you had finished with as your understanding of a problem changes. And you will also find that the final stage of the process, Action-Planning, will often lead you back to the beginning by generating new messes, new opportunities, and new situations that offer problem-solving challenges.

Well, that's the whole process, described from the outside. Now we're going to get inside CPS by using it to solve a real problem in your life.

### *Practice using CPS*

The only way to learn CPS is to practice using it. But let us warn you ahead of time: CPS is not a quick way to solve a problem. It takes time, and if you have a problem that isn't worth spending at least an hour working on — because it doesn't really matter much, or because you think you already have a good solution in mind, or because you're not really in a position to implement *any* kind of solution (which might be the problem you *should* be working on!) — then you shouldn't plan on using CPS.

A good mess to start with is one that is *your* mess — that is, it's a situation in which you are directly involved — and it's a mess that you both care about and one that you don't (yet) know how to solve. It might be a problem with students, a teacher, some colleagues, family, yourself, or a friend; it might be a problem with finances, planning for the future, or finding a job; it might be a problem having to do with a course you're taking, or one you're teaching; it could be almost anything, any situation that you think you would like to improve, whether the situation is one that you currently like but want to make even better, or one that you currently dislike and want to change.

You may have something in mind already, but even if you do, try the Mess-Finding activity that follows. It may help you discover some other messes you can work on another day.

For every step of the process you'll need paper — lots of it — and a pencil or pen. For your first adventure in CPS, space will be provided in this book, but if you find you need more paper don't hesitate to get some. (When you work in a group, lots of newsprint taped to the wall and some kind of markers are indispensable. That way everyone can see all the ideas from each step in the process.) And, as we've said, you'll need time. If you try to rush things, you won't learn CPS well. After you get comfortable with the model, you'll often find that there are steps you can sometimes streamline, but for now, take each step slowly and in order. Of course, if you have some good ideas at a later step that cause you to want to redo your work at earlier steps, by all means do so. Good ideas are too precious to waste.

### *Mess-Finding*

In every step of the process, we'll start by brainstorming. After developing a long list of ideas, we'll then begin to evaluate, narrowing down the list. But remember the brainstorming rules (if you've forgotten, go back to Chapter 2).

You should write down every idea, without regard to the quality of the idea. Evaluation will come later. It's hard not to do some evaluating as you go, of course, but keep this in mind:

> It takes at least a dozen bad ideas to produce one good idea.

So produce all the ideas — bad and good — that you can.

105

What kinds of things should you list under Mess-Finding? Here are some questions you might try to answer:

- What have you done lately that you would like to do better?

- What sort of conflicts have you been having lately?

- What, or who, is bugging you?

- What challenges are on your mind?

- What is your concern about … (some person or persons, or some activity or goal, in your life)?

- What opportunity would you like to take advantage of?

- What opportunity would you like to create for yourself?

- Who has been on your mind? Why?

- What goals do you have for this week, month, or year?

Take some time now to try to generate along list of possible messes. Go beyond the obvious ones, the ones you think of right away. Include some silly ideas — thinking about them often loosens up other, important ideas, and even the silliest of ideas often carries a germ of truth hidden somewhere beneath the surface. When you think you have a full list, try to think of ten more. And maybe ten more beyond that.

_____

_____

_____

_____

_____

_____

_____

_____

_____

_____

# CHAPTER 4

When your list is about as long as you think it will ever be, take time to evaluate and refine it. Which concerns seem most important? What silly ideas can you look at a different way and turn into real concerns? What items on your list are about the same general topic? Can you combine any of these ideas into a new mess?

Work over your list, gradually selecting the potential messes that interest you most. Don't erase anything or scratch anything out beyond recognition — you may need that idea later. It's okay to scratch through things lightly, and to circle or asterisk or otherwise mark the ideas that you think you might actually want to work on.

There's no magic process for selecting a mess. Keep narrowing your list down until you have the mess you want to work on right now — and remember, everything else on the list isn't being ignored, only postponed. If you have a half dozen messes you really want to work on, save five for later and choose one for now.

### Data-Finding

Okay, it's time to brainstorm again. Anything about the mess situation that might possibly be relevant — anything that comes to mind — should go down on paper. This includes feelings, goals, things you know and things you might want to find out, people involved and how they're involved, anything that connects to the situation. And when you run out of ideas, pause and think of the situation in a different way, from a different perspective, perhaps through the eyes of someone else. You want to go beyond the obvious. What matters about the situation, and why?

_____

_____

_____

_____

_____

_____

_____

_____

_____

_____

# CHAPTER 4

When you've listed everything you can think of, go back and review your list. This review will probably remind you of other things that should be on the list, so write down those new ideas. And as you go, circle or in some way highlight the things that you most want to keep in mind as you continue the process. There is no need to scratch through anything — you needn't really narrow down this list to any particular number of items — but make special note of those things that seem especially important, surprising, confusing, or simply interesting. When you do this in a group, there's no need that everyone agree which of the items are most important — you needn't reach consensus about every asterisk — but this review of facts and feelings and goals will help everyone understand everyone else's perspective on the situation.

### *Problem-Finding*

Remember the magic words? "In what ways might I ...?" or "How might I ...?" Every problem statement should begin with one of these phrases. It's okay to use an abbreviation like "I.W.W.M.I. ..." or "H.M.I. ..." (When you do this in a group, of course, the magic words would be "In what ways might we ...?" or "How might we ...?")

What you want to do first is brainstorm as many possible problem statements as you can. Remember *not* to try to solve the problem now or to include solutions in your problem statements. That will be hard to avoid — everyone doing Problem-Finding for the first few times wants to go right to finding solutions. When you find yourself coming up with solutions rather than problem statements, ask yourself "What is the problem that this solution would solve?" and write that down (using either the "In what ways might I" or "How might I" formula, of course).

Try to find general problems that include more specific ones. (Recall the "How might I build a better mousetrap?" example earlier.) Work both ways, trying to come up with more general problem statements and also breaking larger problems into mini-problems, each with its own problem statement. Review your list occasionally as you go, trying to find ways to put two or more of your problem statements together into a single, over-arching problem statement.

This is a very important and tricky step, so take your time. Don't judge your ideas — remember brainstorming rules — but review your list often to help you generate more ideas. You may find it helpful to review your Data-Finding list to help you generate more problem statements. And don't forget to use the magic words to begin *every* problem statement!!

_____

_____

_____

_____

CHAPTER 4

When you think you've looked at the problem from every possible angle, look at it from a few more angles and try to come up with a few more problem statements. Remember, this is a difficult and important problem, and time spent now will usually be paid back later. If you rush this step, you may end up solving the wrong problem, or at least limiting yourself unnecessarily in the ways you might solve it.

When you've finally decided that you have all the different problem statements you can come up with, it's time to evaluate. Remember, it's okay to come up with new ideas as you do this — Just add them to the list. As you lightly scratch through improbable or otherwise weak problem statements, see if there is a way to rescue them. That is, if you have a fanciful or silly problem statement, can you find a way to turn it into a problem statement that you might really want to work on? Your goal is to end up with the very best, most workable problem statement that you can, one that doesn't limit the range of possible solutions unnecessarily or point toward a particular kind of solution.

Gradually weed your list of problem statements down to a few that you especially like. Of the remaining few, is there a way to combine them into one more general problem statement?

Finally, you're going to have to come up with a single problem statement. That doesn't mean the others are wasted, however. They are still there, in the back of your mind, guiding you as you work through the process (and they are still there, on your paper, in case you change your mind later on).

### Idea-Finding

At last it's time to try to come up with solutions. Brainstorming rules apply. Try to think of many, different, and unusual ways to solve the problem. Combine ideas. Write down fanciful, wild, even ridiculous solutions— these often contain just the stimulus your brain needs to unleash the most exciting, and often the best, candidate solutions.

It sometimes happens during Idea-Finding that you come across what seems like a perfect solution and you stop. That's okay, sometimes. But not this time. Keep going, try to find other, different, and possibly even better solutions than your "perfect" one. Make your list long, then make it longer.

_____

_____

_____

_____

_____

_____

115

CHAPTER 4

When you have a list that has many good ideas (and many bad ones — you should have lots of both), it's time to narrow down the possibilities. As always, it's okay to add new ideas, to combine two or more ideas, to revise ideas — in fact, all these things are encouraged. Gradually weed through the list, trying to get it down to a few strong ideas — let's say somewhere between 3 and 8. But don't go further than this. We're not ready yet to pick a *best* solution. That's what the next step is all about.

## Solution-Finding

This is a step that takes lots of patience, because by now you may want to hurry up and pick one of your ideas and run with it. And sometimes that's okay, especially when you're working alone on a problem. But not this time, because it's important to learn how to choose among a set of candidate solutions when you aren't really sure which is best (or when a group is working together, and there's no clear consensus).

As always, the first step is to think of possibilities, after which we will narrow down the list. One place to get ideas for possible criteria is to go back to the problem statement. Here's an example. Let's say the problem statement was, "In what ways might I keep Terry and Wally from fighting in class?" In this case, one might include among possible criteria such things as:

- Will the solution result in less fighting by Terry and Wally?

- Will the solution result in better behavior by Terry and Wally?

- Will the solution result in greater interest in their class work by Terry and Wally?

- Will the solution result in less fighting by all students in my class?

Note that some of these criteria go directly back to the problem statement and others seem to be asking the solution to do things that were not originally part of the problem statement. That's fine, for two reasons:

- This is brainstorming, and any idea is a good idea — Judgment will come later.

- You may want more from a solution than you originally put in your problem statement. It's up to you at this point to decide what the criteria are for a good solution, whether or not those criteria exactly fit the problem statement.

Of course, if you have some insight at this point that leads you to decide that your problem statement really wasn't the problem you want to solve, then you may need to go back a few steps, develop a new problem statement, and then do some Idea-Finding based on *that* statement of the problem.

There are other kinds of criteria that you might list that do not come out of the problem statement, but which might nonetheless be important, such as:

- Will I have time to implement the solution without too much sacrifice of my time or the time of the rest of the class?

- Is the solution fair to Terry, Wally, the rest of the class?

- Can I obtain whatever materials and/or cooperation of others that this solution entails?

- Is the result likely to be worth the difficulty of implementing the solution?

- What "fringe benefits" or unplanned costs/drawbacks are likely to result from implementing the solution?

This list will be different depending on the problem statement, and will to some degree be conditioned by the ideas you know you will need to judge. (After all, you just spent a good bit of time developing that list of ideas.) You probably already have some sense of the strengths and weaknesses of some of your candidate solutions. By what criteria are you getting this sense of what is good and what is bad in those candidate solutions? List those, and many more, criteria. As always, the goal is to list as many *possible* criteria as you can.

Eventually you will need to narrow down your list to the criteria that seem most important to you, and then to use these criteria to guide your selection of a solution (or several solutions, as the case may be). There's no magic way to do this. Some people rate the relative importance of the criteria and give each a weight, such as 1 (least important) to 10 (most important). They then give points on some scale (0-100, 1-10, 1-4? — it doesn't really matter as long as you use the same scale consistently) to each candidate solution for each criterion. Finally they multiply the weight times the points for each candidate solution and each criterion and sum to see which solution gets the most points. The illustration Solution-Finding: Using a Weighted Point System is an example, using three criteria and three possible solutions.

*Solution-Finding: Using a Weighted Point System*

|  | WEIGHT | CANDIDATE SOLUTION 1 | CANDIDATE SOLUTION 2 | CANDIDATE SOLUTION 3 |
|---|---|---|---|---|
| CRITERION 1 | 10 | 3 x 10 = 30 | 4 x 10 = 40 | 2 x 10 = 20 |
| CRITERION 2 | 6 | 2 x 6 = 12 | 2 x 6 = 12 | 4 x 6 = 24 |
| CRITERION 3 | 3 | 4 x 3 = 12 | 1 x 3 = 3 | 3 x 3 = 9 |
| TOTALS |  | 54 | 55 | 53 |

This gives the appearance of being very precise, but all the numbers are actually based on a series of estimates, so the appearance of precision is misleading. We find this method to be generally more cumbersome than helpful, but some people who use CPS regularly find it very useful. Use it if it works for you.

The purpose of developing the criteria for judging is to help you be clearer about what you're looking for in a good solution. This may lead to combining or adjusting some of the candidate solutions, or simply to selecting one or more solutions as they are. If you still cannot decide at this point, don't force it. If you have several good solutions and can't choose among them, take time to imagine in detail how well each would do under each of your criteria. You might try PMI ("Plus-Minus-Interesting," which we looked at in Chapter 2) as a way to help you evaluate your alternatives further and make a choice.

If you don't need to choose among competing ideas — if, for example, you have a number of ideas that you like and you see no obstacle to implementing all of them — then there is really little solution-Finding to be done. It also often happens, especially when working on a problem alone, that a candidate solution seems so good that stopping to evaluate several alternatives would simply be a waste of time. In those instances, if you're sure you have the solution(s) you want, then you should skip the solution-Finding step and move directly from idea-Finding to action-Planning.

On the other hand, if you don't feel that you have any good ideas at all to choose from, then it may be time to go back to an earlier step in the process and try again.

You might want to do some more idea-Finding, or you might want to go back to problem-Finding and look for a new way to think about the situation.

*Action-Planning*

Whose help will you need to implement your solution? What materials or other resources? What resistance or other obstacles do you envision? Are there different phases of implementation? When will you begin? What is a reasonable timeline? How will you assess progress along the way?

These are some of the questions that you need to ask yourself as part of action planning. The basic strategy is the same: List all the things that you might need to do as part of implementing your solution. Answering the questions in the preceding paragraph is a start, but for every problem and solution the questions will be different.

# CHAPTER 4

In many cases, Action-Planning will help you further refine your solution as you begin to spell out your solution in detail. Some of the ideas that result from the brainstorming phase of Action-Planning will be more important than others, and some may become new messes that you'll want to use CPS to solve.

Back when we were Mess-Finding, the instructions were pretty much the same for everyone, but as you move through the steps, each problem (and each problem solver) follows a unique path. By the time you reach Action-Planning, there are very few general directions one can give that will fit all situations. Keep in mind the goals of Action-Planning: to develop a specific plan of action and a time table for the plan, to identify likely obstacles and to plan how to overcome them, and to plan how to evaluate the effectiveness of the solution.

*Where to go from here*

CPS is something for you to use to solve real problems. Practice using CPS will not make you a perfect problem solver — there is no such thing — but the more you practice the better you will become at solving a variety of problems. So what you should do now is use CPS to find many messes and to solve many problems!

Should you teach CPS to your students? That depends on their age and on how much time you are willing to spend working with them to improve their problem solving skills. Generally it's hard for primary-grade students to keep the full model in mind, and we do not recommend actually teaching them CPS as such. It is better, we believe, to model this kind of thinking; to practice divergent and evaluative thinking skills (which are the nuts and bolts on each step of CPS); and to use CPS when working with students in groups or individually to solve tough problems, but without actually referring to the model.

If you plan to teach older students CPS, we recommend doing it just the way we have taught you. Introduce the model, explain each of the steps, and then have each student use the CPS steps to work on a tough personal problem. Then remind them to use CPS, provide opportunities for using it (such as long-term projects like science fair experiments), and model CPS in your own problem solving.

Finally, don't force CPS. Try to present it in a way that makes it seem more like fun than work. Remember that CPS is not for every problem, and that not everyone is ready to learn CPS.

And for yourself, use CPS to solve real problems and practice using CPS to become a more skillful problem solver, but don't lose sight of the fact that most of the things you do when you use CPS are actually very interesting. The more you enjoy doing CPS — especially the divergent-thinking, brainstorming first part of each step in the process — the more creative your problem solving is likely to be. And the more fun you'll have!

## BIBLIOGRAPHY

The CPS model presented here is based on modifications to the earlier Osborn-Parnes CPS model as described in S.G. Isaksen & D.J. Treffinger's *Creative*

*Problem Solving: The Basic Course* (Bearly Ltd., 1985). Two excellent sources of further information on CPS are Isaksen, Dorval, & Treffinger's *Creative Approaches to Problem Solving* (Kendall-Hunt, 1994) and Treffinger, Isaksen, & Dorval's *Creative Problem Solving: An Introduction* (Center for Creative Learning, 1994). Any of these books will help you extend your understanding of CPS.

One of John's favorite books is Eberle and Stanish's *CPS for Kids: A Resource Book of Teaching Creative Problem Solving*, which we already recommended at the end of Chapter 2. It provides exercises that young students can use to practice each step of CPS. This is worthwhile practice, even though we don't recommend teaching young students the whole model as such. If students learn the skills that are part of each step, they will be more creative thinkers, and they will also be prepared when they are older to put it all together into a complete problem solving model.

All the other references at the end of Chapter 2 could also be useful here, as divergent thinking is a key part of CPS. Unfortunately there is far less literature available to help you and your students practice the other kinds of skills important in CPS, evaluative thinking.

If you want to continue your study of CPS, you might want to attend the week-long Creative Problem Solving Institute held each June. It is sponsored by the Creative Education Foundation (http://www.creativeeducationfoundation.org/).

Finally, if you are looking for evidence of the impact of CPS training, John assessed the long-term impact of CPS training with groups of eighth-grade students and wrote up his research in an article entitled "Long-Term Effects of Creativity Training With Middle School Students" (*Journal of Early Adolescence*, 1988, volume 8, pp. 183-193). What he found, in summary, was that even after sixth months students trained in CPS were much more effective at solving real-world kinds of problems than similar students who had not had such training.

Most important, however, is that you use CPS regularly. Reading about it may be helpful, but you can learn CPS only if you actually *practice* CPS. Use the guidelines in this chapter, and refer to them often so that you don't skip or inadvertently change important steps in the process.

## SUMMING UP

This chapter will begin by summarizing a few of the most important ideas that have been discussed thus far. Next we'll look at some ways these ideas intersect one another, especially in a classroom context. And finally, you'll be asked to think about some issues that relate to how you might implement these ideas in your classroom.

### A review

The three main topics of this book — divergent thinking, intrinsic motivation, and CPS — do not cover everything that is known about creativity. Even if one includes some of the book's important subtopics like task specificity, creativity testing, and evaluative thinking, much remains to be said about creativity. The lists of references at the end of each chapter will help readers who want to dig deeper into the creativity literature.

This book does, however, explain most of what is known about creativity that is directly applicable to creativity training. If you practice and teach divergent thinking (in a task-specific way, of course), using brainstorming and other idea-generating techniques; if you manage your own motivations and the goal structures in your classroom to maximize intrinsic motivation when your goal is creative thinking, while at the same time using extrinsic motivation to learn and teach skills and to help keep yourself and your students going when intrinsic motivation begins to flag; and if you use and teach the CPS model of creative problem solving to work on the most challenging situations that you encounter — if you do these things, then you, and your students, will become much more creative in the way you think and in the things you do. And not only will you become a more creative teacher of more creative students: You and you students will also enjoy the things you do more than you ever have before.

We've picked out five topics for a quick review. Readers who turned directly to this chapter without reading the first four chapters will probably be disappointed; these are not things that one can learn without thinking rather deeply about them, and this quick review will not afford that opportunity. Of course, if you turned back here for a *pre*view before reading the full book, then this chapter may serve to whet your appetite, and you have our permission to read on.

And for those of you who have read and thought deeply about the various topics discusses in Chapters 1 through 4, we hope this review will be both a reminder of what you've learned and a stimulus to think some more about each of these ideas. The five topics to be reviewed are: divergent thinking, task specificity, creativity testing, intrinsic motivation, and the CPS model of problem solving.

*Divergent thinking*

One of the most important skills underlying creativity is divergent thinking. Divergent thinking refers to the generation of many different and unusual ideas in response to a given situation. There are four component skills that make up divergent thinking:

- *Fluency* is the ability to generate a large *number* of ideas.

- *Flexibility* is the ability to generate a wide *variety* of ideas.

- *Originality* is the ability to generate *unusual* ideas.

*Elaboration* is the ability to generate many *details* to expand and enrich one's ideas.

Brainstorming is the most important method of producing divergent thinking. Although the term "brainstorming" has become a common one, it is often used to refer to situations or skills that are very different from the very specific technique for generating ideas that is the original meaning of the term "brainstorming." When people have good idea they may refer to them as brainstorms, or they may say they are brainstorming a topic only to mean that they are thinking hard about something. But these are not the same as the divergent thinking *technique* brainstorming.

Brainstorming follows four rules designed to increase one's divergent thinking production. The rules are:

Defer judgment. To defer does not mean avoid evaluation, only to postpone it. Evaluation of ideas should occur *after* one has finished, for the time being, trying to produce new ideas. Concurrent production and evaluation of ideas tends to lead to fewer, less interesting, and less imaginative ideas.

Avoid ownership of ideas. This is mainly an issue when a group is brainstorming together. (Individual brainstorming is sometimes called "brainwriting," but it is otherwise the same.) It is easy for egos to get in the way of creative thinking, and if ideas are "owned" by whoever suggests them during brainstorming, that person may be more reluctant to let them be fairly evaluated at a later stage. Similarly, others may be reluctant to criticize ideas "owned" by someone else for fear of hurting the feelings of that person.

Feel free to "hitchhike" on other ideas. This is related to rule 2 about not owning ideas, but it goes further in reminding us that every idea needn't be a totally unique creation. It's okay to borrow elements from ideas already on the table, or to make slight modifications of ideas already suggested.

Wild ideas are encouraged. This is something of an extension of rule 1 about deferring judgment, because valuing wild ideas remind us forcefully of the "anything goes" atmosphere that is conducive to good divergent thinking. Impossible, amusing, or totally unworkable ideas are sometimes just the lubrication needed to make possible the production of workable, but original or highly unusual, ideas. And it's generally easier to take a wildly imaginative bad idea and tone it down to fit the constraints of reality than to take a boring bad idea and make it interesting enough to be worth thinking about.

Divergent thinking is a very important part of creativity, and we know a great deal about how to improve divergent thinking skills. *Divergent thinking is not the same thing as creativity*, however, and neither is it the only important creativity-relevant thinking skill. Evaluative thinking, which typically follows divergent thinking, is one other important creative thinking skill discussed in the book. Other skills that are important in creative performance are often skills that are not uniquely associated with creativity, such as knowledge of the vocabulary and important ideas in a given domain, skill using techniques commonly employed in a domain, exemplars of highly respected products in a domain, etc. This kind of knowledge, technical skill, and awareness of standards is often very task specific, as is divergent thinking.

### Task specificity

There are some people who are creative in a wide variety of domains — people who can solve all kinds of problems, invent wonderful new recipes, write imaginative stories, design interesting experiments to test scientific hypotheses, show uncanny insight in interpreting the behavior of others, etc. — and there are also people who show little of what most people would deem creative thinking. But even if creative talent in different fields were randomly distributed, this is exactly what we would expect: Some people would have many different talents, some people would have very few, and most people would have some mixture of higher creativity in some areas and lower creativity in others.

Whether we are looking at creative genius or the more garden-variety creativity that has been the focus of this book, it appears that people's creativity varies greatly from task to task. Creativity researchers have not yet reached full consensus on the issue of task specificity, but the tide is currently moving in that direction. In the meantime, for reasons explained in Chapter 2, it is wise for those interested in becoming more creative and in improving the creative thinking skills of their students to act as if the task specificity theory is the correct one.

Understanding task specificity is especially important in the training of divergent thinking skills. If you are interested in improving your creative thinking primarily in one area, then you should concentrate on divergent thinking exercises that use only that task domain for their content. But if you want to increase creative thinking skill across a wide variety of areas, then the divergent thinking exercises you use should draw on a wide variety of content.

### Creativity testing

Almost all creative thinking tests are actually tests of divergent thinking skills. This is a limitation, because divergent thinking is just one part of creativity. But it's an important part, and if divergent thinking tests were valid tests of some kind of general-purpose divergent thinking skills, then they would tell us something important about an individual's creative potential. Unfortunately, the problems with these tests run deep, making them of little value in assessing such potential.

One problem with these divergent thinking tests is that it is easy to teach people how to improve their scores significantly on them, even without knowing what questions will be on the test or even which divergent thinking test one will be taking. If the stakes are high — such as admission to desirable school programs — then those who have been coached can have a large advantage. The impact of coaching on divergent thinking test scores is much larger than the advantage enjoyed by college-bound students who take commercial SAT prep courses. And effective divergent thinking test coaching can be accomplished in under an hour.

Another problem is the probable task specificity of divergent thinking. Even if divergent thinking tests were reliable and valid measures of a particular kind of divergent thinking — for example, divergent thinking skill in inventing new ways to advertise a product — that wouldn't say anything about divergent thinking skill in other areas such as graphic arts, science, or poetry.

If you must use divergent thinking tests of some kind, then it would be prudent to try to match the test to the kind of divergent thinking skill you are most interested in. For example, if "creativity" is one criterion for admission to a gifted/talented program, and if the program mostly concentrates on creative writing, then a test that has students come up with such things such as ways to use a brick would be less helpful than one that asked for a list of ways a character might handle a given situation. For example, the task might be to make a list of different ways a person might propose marriage. (Perhaps this kind of activity was the genesis of Paul Simon's hit song, "Fifty Ways to Leave Your Lover.")

There is a better kind of test of creativity, however, which goes beyond measuring divergent thinking skill. This technique is the assessment of the creativity of actual products. If you are using a test to determine admission to a creative writing program, for example, simply have students write stories and then have those stories rated for creativity by experts (who don't know the identity of the students, of course). This kind of "authentic" testing is becoming increasingly popular in all manner of assessment, and it's hard to think of an area in which it is more appropriate than creativity. However, one still must remember that creativity-relevant skills tend to be quite task specific. Using creativity ratings of stories for admission to a program in science wouldn't make sense.

### Intrinsic motivation

The idea that we are more creative when we find something intrinsically interesting is an easy one to grasp, at least at first. As we saw in Chapter 3, it becomes complicated when we learn that extrinsic constraints (such as expecting that your work will be evaluated, or taking on a task in order to earn a reward) tend to drive out intrinsic motivation. This often puts teachers in the position of having to decide what one's immediate goals are — Is it important that students learn some skill? Or is it more important to encourage their creativity? — and then trying to design goal structures conducive to either extrinsic or intrinsic motivation.

It's far easier to induce extrinsic motivation than to create intrinsic motivation. Because extrinsic motivation tends to drive out intrinsic motivation, it's also fairly easy to decrease intrinsic motivation, but hard to increase it. But it's not impossible. Allowing students to make choices, reminding them of interesting aspects of a project, and planning activities that tap into students' interests are a few common ways teachers do this.

It's also possible to de-emphasize the extrinsic constraints that are typically very salient in classrooms. Requiring students to do certain assignments but promising not to evaluate their work is one way. Having students work in cooperative groups, but structuring the activity in ways that neither encourage competition among the groups nor emphasize rewards for superior performance is another. Of course, if the activities themselves are interesting to students, it is much easier to dispense with extrinsic constraints.

But much of the time in most classrooms, short-term creative performance in not the goal of a lesson, and both evaluation and rewards are appropriate. Some behaviors just won't happen unless students are offered rewards. And to develop skills — skills which may be employed, in the future, in creative work — students need feedback on the quality of their work. When in providing such feedback, however, focusing on the work itself and not the abilities of the student who did the work is generally better because it causes less of a decrease in intrinsic motivation and creativity.

Both skill-oriented lessons and creativity-oriented lessons should be part of every classroom. Good teaching often means providing a balance of goal structures and emphasizing different kinds of motivation in your classroom at different times. While evaluation and rewards remain important tools of our trade, not *every* activity should be evaluated or done for a reward.

Finally, we can do a great deal to manipulate our own motivations in positive and productive ways. Some days the joys of teaching are too obvious to miss, but other days we may need to remind ourselves what is interesting, enjoyable, and pleasantly exciting about teaching to boost our intrinsic motivation (as well as our creativity and our pleasure in teaching). Other times — like evenings when there is a pile of ungraded essays waiting for our attention — we may need to use extrinsic motivation just to keep us going, perhaps by reminding ourselves how good we will feel to finish the job, or even "bribing" ourselves by promising to go out for a sundae as soon as those papers are graded. And we can teach our students to manage their own motivations as well.

*CPS*

The best way to learn CPS is to practice CPS. We won't review the steps here, but we want to emphasize again the importance of one step in the process: problem-Finding. After data-Finding, people often want to rush past problem-Finding to begin thinking of possible solutions. Taking time to generate many ideas in the problem-Finding stage and using the "magic" formats: "In what ways might we …?" or "How might we …?" are part of the sometimes surprising power of CPS. This stage is often the most important part of problem solving precisely because it encourages us to look at a problem in different ways, not the same way we may have been looking at it (unsuccessfully) for a long time.

CPS takes time, and if you need an answer in a hurry, or if you simply don't have the patience at the moment, then it's not a good time to launch into full-blown CPS-style problem solving. (John once saw a cartoon of two plumbers standing outside a door which had a sign "CPS session in progress." Water is gushing out of the room, and it's already knee-deep in the hallway. One of the plumbers says, "They're probably somewhere between 'In what ways might we turn off the faucets?' and 'How might we filter the water for swimming?'" CPS is simply not an appropriate tool when prompt action is needed.)

CPS alternates between divergent thinking and evaluative thinking, which reminds us of the importance of both in creativity. In this book there is no chapter devoted exclusively to improving one's evaluative thinking skills, although there some techniques are introduced that will do just that. Plus-Minus-Interesting is essentially a method of evaluative thinking. It appears in Chapter 2 because it is an activity that employs divergent thinking in the service of evaluation. And in Chapter 4's CPS solution-Finding section there is a technique which uses weighted criteria to help evaluate and choose among competing ideas. But divergent thinking gets more attention than evaluative thinking. There are two reasons for this:

> It is unlikely that divergent thinking will be encouraged in classrooms unless a teacher explicitly sets out to do so. Evaluative thinking, on the other hand, is more commonly emphasized in textbooks and course objectives.

We have a great deal more knowledge, based on empirical research, to tell us how to go about improving divergent thinking skills.

In CPS, divergent thinking is followed, at each stage of the process, by evaluative thinking. But evaluation need not always follow idea generation. It is worth practicing divergent thinking just for the practice. It is also a useful tool to use when starting a new activity, both to get a sense of what students know and to generate interest in the topic. In those cases, there is no need for divergent thinking to be followed by evaluative thinking.

If one uses divergent thinking as part of a problem-solving process, however, it is natural to follow divergent thinking with evaluative thinking, just as the CPS model prescribes (even if you are not following the full CPS model). It is good problem solving to do this, and it will also provide both divergent thinking and evaluative thinking practice.

## WHERE DIVERGENT THINKING, INTRINSIC MOTIVATION, AND CPS INTERSECT

### Divergent thinking and CPS

This connection is a rather obvious one, and we won't belabor it here. Divergent thinking is part of CPS, and developing divergent thinking skill will improve one's CPS skill. Using CPS will, in turn, enhance one's skill in divergent thinking.

### Divergent thinking and intrinsic motivation

Using divergent thinking as an introductory activity to some topic of study will, among other things, tend to increase students' interest in the topic. This happens because students are reminded of what they know about the topic (that is, their prior knowledge is activated) and because they get a taste of what's to come by hearing some things other students know about it. Because divergent thinking is done in a non-evaluative atmosphere, it does not encourage the kind of evaluation- and reward-driven extrinsic motivation that tends to overwhelm student's intrinsic interest in a subject. Conversely, using things that have intrinsic interest for students as divergent thinking practice topics will tend to make those divergent thinking practice sessions more interesting, enjoyable, and productive.

### Intrinsic motivation and CPS

CPS can take a long time, and although it can be very enjoyable, it is not for the faint of heart or the easily distracted. CPS requires far more time and energy than, say, a single brainstorming activity, and it therefore requires more motivation. That motivation may be both intrinsic (e.g., because the topic is an interesting one, or because of the intrinsic reward of accomplishment you will get by solving this particular problem) and extrinsic (e.g., because there will be some reward for solving the problem, or because your solution may be evaluated by others). Most situations, especially the complex situations one typically is dealing with when using CPS, involve both intrinsically and extrinsically motivating aspects.

You will be more successful in teaching CPS if the problems you work on are interesting to your students. And even when they are not, it is worth trying to massage the groups' motivations at times by reminding them — or having them try to remind each other — what about this problem *is* interesting, even if at the moment it may feel more like work than play. This will help raise everyone's levels of intrinsic motivation, which will, in turn, enhance the creativity of the group.

### Creativity and your classroom

We have a few more brainstorming activities for you to do that will help you begin putting the ideas in this book to work in your classroom (or, if you are not currently teaching, in the classroom you imagine yourself teaching in soon). The first one is a brainstorming activity, which you will note is framed in the magic words of problem finding: *In what ways might I use divergent thinking, intrinsic motivation, and CPS in my classroom?*

Remember the rules of brainstorming and don't judge ideas as they come to you, just write them down. And go for wild, impossible ideas as well as tame, easily imaginable ones. The question is a wide-open one, one you probably have been thinking about off and on as you've read this book. Write down all those ideas that you already have in mind, and try to generate many, many more!

*In what ways might I use divergent thinking, intrinsic motivation, and CPS in my classroom?*

# CHAPTER 5

Take a moment now that you've made this list to go back through it and pick out some of the most promising or interesting ideas. There's no need to cross anything out, but you might want to put a mark next to some of what seem at this point like ideas you would really like to pursue. That's as far as we're going to take evaluation, as the actual choice of ideas will probably include many items from your list. You will want to continue to develop this list as you begin to put some of its ideas into practice.

The next brainstorming topic is this: *What obstacles do I foresee in putting any of the ideas I like into practice?* These could be very practical concerns or philosophical ones. Different ideas from your first list will generate different ideas about possible obstacles. Include any possible obstacles that you foresee on this list, and don't worry about the order of the items you list, or if the list seems terribly pessimistic. We'll try to turn that pessimism around after you finish this list.

*What obstacles do I foresee in putting any of the ideas I like into practice?*

_____

_____

_____

_____

_____

_____

_____

_____

_____

_____

_____

_____

_____

_____

_____

_____

_____

_____

_____

_____

_____

_____

_____

_____

_____

_____

CHAPTER 5

Now go through this list and note the possible obstacles that most concern you. There's no set number: It may be only one major obstacle, or it may be many. Mark as many as you wish.

The last brainstorming topic is this: *In what ways might I overcome any of the obstacles on my list?* This might include changing actual things, or opinions of others, or even your own views. Is it possible to turn any of these obstacles into opportunities? Your list can include ideas relating to any obstacle you listed (even those you didn't mark but want to include), and don't worry about the order in which you list them.

———————————

*In what ways might I overcome any of the obstacles on my list?*

———————————————————————————

———————————————————————————

———————————————————————————

———————————————————————————

———————————————————————————

———————————————————————————

———————————————————————————

———————————————————————————

———————————————————————————

———————————————————————————

———————————————————————————

———————————————————————————

———————————————————————————

———————————————————————————

———————————————————————————

———————————————————————————

———————————————————————————

———————————————————————————

CHAPTER 5

# CHAPTER 5

## A FINAL WORD

We hope that you can think of many ways to use the ideas in this book to help you improve your own creative thinking skills and those of your students. We're sure you will encounter obstacles; we are equally sure you will find ways to overcome most of those obstacles.

John has for many years had a sign over my desk that says "Good problem solvers see opportunities where others see only problems." It's a philosophy that we both like, one that we probably haven't always lived up to, but one that we have certainly aspired to live by. It's an ideal philosophy for bringing more creativity into your life, and we hope you will find it as helpful and inspiring as we have.

CHAPTER 6

## CAN TEACHING FOR CREATIVITY AND TEACHING FOR CONTENT KNOWLEDGE MIX?

### AN EASY QUESTION

If you want to remember something, will you remember it better (a) if you simply read about it or (b) if you think about it actively and in different ways and connect it to other things you already know?

We all know that thinking actively about something promotes recall and understanding. Thinking actively about an idea will usually embed it deeper into the propositional network of our memory than will thinking passively about the same idea; this will lead to better recall later on. We hope you can see where this is leading — and why we are going to argue that teaching for creativity and teaching for content knowledge should not be viewed as antithetical. Rather than being constantly at odds, they very often complement each other. Thinking creatively about something will lead to better understanding. Indeed, this actually works both ways, because acquiring content knowledge also aids creative thinking. But we're not Pollyannas; we know that there can sometimes be conflicts between teaching for creativity and teaching for content knowledge acquisition. This chapter is about how to use potential synergies between the two kinds of teaching. It's also about how to best navigate the inevitable conflicts that sometimes arise between them.

### *Introduction: Squaring the circle*

Ancient geometers set for themselves the task of squaring the circle — constructing a square with the same area as a given circle in a finite number of steps using only a compass and straightedge. If the circle and the square were superimposed, the area of the corners of the square that protrude outside the circle and area of the arcs of the circle that protrude outside the square should then also be the same. It seemed it should be possible, and they did come close, but in 1882 someone proved that this is actually an impossible problem.

Are teaching for creativity and teaching for skill acquisition and content knowledge fundamentally at odds? Is trying to do both like trying to square the circle? There has been a concerted effort in schools in recent years to teach (and to test) content knowledge; at the extreme, schools gear their entire curricular strategies toward the information required to do well on the standardized tests. The recent movement in education toward ever more detailed content standards and accountability has led to concern that students' creativity may suffer as a result.

In our discussion of intrinsic motivation we noted that there are times when teaching for creativity and teaching for knowledge acquisition or skill building can be in conflict. To promote creativity, we generally want to encourage intrinsic motivation and downplay extrinsic motivation. We want to focus on what is interesting or meaningful and avoid rewards, evaluations, and the like.

But in many ways, creativity *requires* content knowledge. Many researchers, such as Dean Keith Simonton and Howard Gardner, argue for a "ten year" rule. Such a rule states that it takes ten years after entering a field (any field) to make a significant contribution. These ten years can be spent learning the mechanics of the field, discovering all of the practical issues that typically are not taught, and continued deliberate practice. These ten years do not represent a basic apprenticeship. Rather, these are years of active experimentation and new ideas. Obviously, we are not focused on "significant contributions" to a field when we are teaching in the classroom — but the role of content knowledge in higher levels of creativity can also speak to everyday creativity.

In addition, thinking deeply (and creatively) about a topic often helps cement one's knowledge of that topic. So increasing students' content knowledge can help them be more creative, and encouraging them to think creatively about the content they are studying will make it more like they will recall that information later. The two can go hand-in-hand.

Even such specific creativity-relevant skills as divergent thinking can be employed in ways that both increase creativity and knowledge of specific content (something we discussed briefly in the chapter about divergent thinking). As we mentioned, however, classroom practices that encourage extrinsic motivation represent one area in which teaching for creativity and teaching content knowledge are often in direct opposition, and we don't intend to pretend this is never a problem. It is unrealistic to pretend that we don't need extrinsic constraints like rewards and critical evaluations of student work, both of which can help students gain content knowledge but which tend to depress creativity. There are ways to employ rewards and evaluations judiciously that will allow teachers to help students become more creative thinkers, however, while also acquiring important domain-specific skills and content knowledge. What we know about how to do those things comprise the focus of this chapter.

Some of the techniques we discuss later in this chapter, and even some of the examples, are ones discussed in earlier chapters about divergent thinking and intrinsic motivation. The difference is that in this chapter we will show how to use these techniques in ways that promote not only creative thinking but the acquisition of skills and content knowledge as well.

Like efforts to square the circle, there is no perfect way to combine teaching for creativity and teaching for skill and knowledge acquisition. But nothing in teaching is ever perfect — we are teachers working with complex minds and complex ideas, not geometers working with only with compasses and straightedges — and coming close to perfection in teaching would be success indeed. There are some inevitable conflicts between teaching for creativity and teaching for content knowledge acquisition, but they can be minimized, and there are also many ways these two goals can work together and support each other. So we can't square the circle, but like the ancient geometers, we can come close.

## Some background

There is a movement in education toward more explicit and detailed content standards. This movement includes both state initiatives and nation-wide efforts like the Core Knowledge Foundation's Core Knowledge Sequence. The perceived need for accountability is a major impetus behind this movement.

There is a sense among many educators that the push for stricter content standards will decrease the amount of time teachers can allocate to the teaching of thinking skills, and especially creativity. The philosopher Richard Paul has gone so far as to suggest that a focus on the acquisition of content knowledge might turn students into "informational blotters." There is also a concern that content standards will encourage teachers to limit their instruction to that which will be tested.

Does the rush to embrace strict content standards mean that developing students' creativity has become an untenable, or at least an unrealistic, objective? Are the goals of developing students' creativity and of meeting specific content standards at odds? We don't have all the empirical evidence we would like to have before answering these questions, and much of the evidence we do have is indirect. Taken together, however, the large amount of indirect evidence that is currently available makes a rather compelling case. The answer to both of these questions seems to be, as it so often is in education, "It depends."

The potential conflict between creativity and content is part of the larger question of the relationship of learning content and learning to think more effectively. It is also related to questions about the possibilities of transfer of learning and of teaching to promote such transfer. We won't pretend that all those disputes have been settled. It seems safe to assert, however, that content knowledge is essential to thinking, that teaching thinking skills must be linked to teaching content in some way, that higher-level thinking typically requires the use of many lower-level skills, and that to improve students' thinking in a given domain, students must acquire an understanding of a lot of factual content about that domain as well as a various domain-specific cognitive skills. So we are pretty sure that:

> thinking depends quite heavily on knowledge mistakes in everyday critical thinking are quite often the result of faulty premises (i.e., incorrect factual knowledge), not a lack of general problem-solving skills, and teaching for transfer requires a great deal of context-specific training or practice in any domain to which transfer is desired.

So in order to improve students' thinking, we have to teach them content knowledge. It's not one or the other, but both. And looked at from the opposite direction, you might say, it is also often true that the best way to teach content knowledge is to get students to think about it in some way — to become actively engaged with the content to be learned. These are very consistent findings of cognitive and educational psychology, although these facts by themselves don't tell us how to do these things. Squaring the circle is still difficult.

No one, not even the most committed advocate of content standards in education, is arguing in favor of the mindless rote memorization of unconnected facts. Pretty much everyone agrees that learning requires that students construct or create meaning in their own minds. Being actively engaged with the content to be learned means active *cognitive* engagement, of course, but the mere awareness of this need for active cognitive engagement tells us nothing about the comparative advantages or disadvantages of any specific method of teaching. An emphasis on content knowledge does not conflict with an emphasis on active processing of information; in fact, the former requires the latter.

So the fact that content standards have become such a powerful force in education need not be bad news to those who wish to emphasize the development of students' thinking skills. The two can go hand in glove, even if at times an artificial rivalry between the two has been proposed by those who have tried to use that false dichotomy as a way to proselytize for some teaching innovation or another. But what about creativity? Surely curriculum content standards — which require, in large part, learning what has already been discovered or created in the past — must interfere with the development of creative thinking in our students?

In many ways, the implication of focusing on content knowledge and skills is the same for creativity as it is for other kinds of thinking. Having richer and more extensive content knowledge and skills should support, not detract from, creative thinking, just as such knowledge and skills support other kinds of thinking. There is a consensus among creativity researchers and theorists that creative genius in particular requires extensive content knowledge. As psychology's prolific historian of creative genius, Dean Keith Simonton (1994), wrote: "There are no shortcuts to greatness. A person who aims to achieve anything of worth must learn, study, and practice" (p. 68).

What of the more everyday or garden-variety creativity that all of us (and our students) share to varying degrees? Once again, domain-specific knowledge and skills appear to be crucial. It appears that most, if not all, of our creative-thinking abilities are fairly narrow in their application. Creative thinking needs content knowledge.

The big question is how to teach content knowledge while *also* teaching creative thinking. Yes, creativity requires content knowledge, but that isn't all it requires. We can't just say, "Well, because creativity requires content knowledge, we can just teach content and not worry about creativity." We still need to focus, at least part of the time, on teaching creative thinking. Here's how to do it, using the tools already introduced in the previous chapters, while also promoting the acquisition of content knowledge.

### Teaching divergent thinking in content areas

It is certainly unlikely that brainstorming possible uses for a brick will increase students' content knowledge, and one might therefore argue that time spent on such activities is simply taking away from time that might be spent on more productive, content-related instruction. But brainstorming and other creativity-relevant activities can easily be connected to relevant content.

Here's an example taken from the New Jersey Core Curriculum Content Standards, which states that students "will acquire geographical understanding by studying the environment and society," and will be able to "explain and predict how the physical environment can accommodate, and be affected by human activity." Most social studies content standards have something along these lines.

These standards relate to a particular geography activity that John used to do with his middle-school social studies students. We introduced this activity back in Chapter 2 but now want to put a different spin on it. The project was to create a new continent somewhere on the globe and to explain how it might have developed culturally. This was an extended project with several lessons on different topics along the way — it took quite a few class periods to complete — but the general goal was to help students understand how geography and human history interact (e.g., how such things as landforms, climate, and waterways influence the things people do and how they do them, and how the things people do and the ways they do them might be adapted to differing geographical settings). This is primarily content knowledge acquisition — and it would help students "acquire geographical understanding by studying the environment and society," and learn how to "explain and predict how the physical environment can accommodate, and be affected by human activity."

John also wanted to use the activity as a way to encourage students' creativity. With that end in mind, he started off with some exercises designed to improve some divergent-thinking skills that students might find useful as they worked on the project. Here are three abilities that he thought might help them make their projects more creative:

Ability to think of specific cultural elements that might be influenced by geography

Ability to think of ways that geography might influence general features of a culture
Ability to think of ways that a people's culture might lead them to adapt different geographical elements to a given purpose

Each of these provided content for brainstorming exercises. For example, after explaining what he meant by "specific cultural elements," he first asked students to brainstorm and create lists of things that might count as cultural elements. This is a direct use of brainstorming to get students to think about content knowledge, and the fact that it is a brainstorming activity doesn't sacrifice the need to teach content knowledge because it does both simultaneously. Because brainstorming engages students, it is far more likely to help them understand what "cultural elements" means than simply lecturing about it or having them read their textbooks. Later he had them brainstorm cultural elements that might be influenced by geography, pushing the idea deeper (and again helping develop their divergent thinking muscles at the same time!).

Evaluation of their ideas generally followed these brainstorming sessions, providing another chance to grapple with important knowledge and skills. These activities — and similar activities related to abilities 2 and 3 above — were designed to increase students' divergent-thinking skill in these particular social studies content areas. Development of these divergent-thinking skills supported the larger create-a-continent activity, and they would also have supported New Jersey Core Curriculum Content Standards. This is a win-win, and is the kind of thing you can do with all kinds of content.

Here's a different example related to teaching mathematics, one that can be used with a wide variety of mathematics topics. When students are confronted with a challenging word problem, it can be helpful to brainstorm possible approaches to solving the problem before doing anything else. Students all too often rush to apply a familiar algorithm, and taking time to brainstorm possible approaches can help them think about and understand the problem before launching into a possibly ill-advised attempt to solve it. The key to solving many word problems is discovering the not-so-obvious structure of the problem. Brainstorming different approaches before deciding how to attack a problem can help students better understand the structure of a problem and what might be needed to solve it.

Brainstorming can also be useful when introducing new concepts in a mathematics class. For example, when introducing triangles for the first time, the teacher might ask students to brainstorm what they know (or think they know) about triangles. This will help activate background knowledge about triangles, and it will also uncover misconception students might have (such as "triangles have three equal sides"). Remember when brainstorming that there are no wrong answers — every idea students suggest should be part of the list — but then after brainstorming the teacher can go back over the list and point out misconceptions and irrelevant ideas (as well as emphasize the useful, appropriate, and accurate ones).

### Intrinsic motivation and creativity

As described above, the goals of helping students gain a wide range of task-specific divergent-thinking skills and helping them learn specific content seem to work well together, as is generally the case with the development of thinking skills and the acquisition of factual content knowledge. There is one area in which teaching for creativity and teaching for content do sometimes conflict, however. As explained in Chapter 3, when it comes to the kinds of motivational constraints one might want to use in the classroom, the goals of teaching or creativity and teaching for knowledge and skill acquisition are sometimes at loggerheads.

As a reminder, here's what the intrinsic motivation theory of creativity says:

> People are more creative when they do something simply because they find it intrinsically interesting — that is, it is something they have chosen to do just because they derive pleasure, or even joy, from doing it — and they are less creative when they do something because they are extrinsically motivated, such as to earn a reward.

So far, so good; this seems pretty harmless, perhaps even obvious, at first blush. But this theory isn't just saying that being intrinsically motivated leads to more creative behavior. It's also saying that when people do things in order to earn rewards, they become less creative; when they do things that they think will be evaluated in some way, they become less creative; and when they do things to please someone else, they become less creative. In fact, many of the things teachers do every day — things most teachers think are essential parts of what they do — decrease students' creativity. That isn't harmless. It seems to call for a total change to the ways schools operate.

As we showed in Chapter 3, creativity does indeed blossom when students feel intrinsically motivated, but they also need to learn a lot of content knowledge and skills if they are to grow creatively. Even for teachers who care deeply about their students' creativity, nurturing students' imaginations isn't the only thing that needs to be done, and promoting intrinsic motivation is but one of several educational goals. Indeed, these goals can sometimes compete and can sometimes work more synergistically.

Here's the bad news in a nutshell: We know that intrinsic and extrinsic motivation tend to compete within us, and when they are both present, intrinsic motivation is generally the loser. Extrinsic motivation tends to drive out intrinsic motivation. That's part of human nature. When we offer our students rewards for doing things, or when we evaluate our students' work, we are both increasing their extrinsic motivation *and* driving out or diminishing their intrinsic motivation for those activities. We are making the things they once found interesting become *less* interesting, less worth doing for their own sake. We are also causing them to be less creative in the ways they perform those activities.

In many ways it would make our jobs simpler if we could just decide no longer to evaluate students' work and to give up offering rewards of any kind, but that isn't really feasible. It would make it difficult — probably impossible — to do much of what we know we must do as teachers, including teaching our students the skills and content that we know they need to learn. Unfortunately, the same things that tend to diminish creativity — extrinsic motivators like rewards and a focus on evaluation — are the very things that tend to increase competence. Students need feedback on their performance to improve their skills (and feedback is a kind of evaluation), and they often need some kind of extrinsic motivation, like rewards, to keep working when they otherwise would simply stop. So they very often need extrinsic motivation to learn.

This is where teaching for creativity and teaching to learn content seem to part company. And for those of us who care about both developing students' creativity and helping students acquire a broad background of content knowledge, this divergence sometimes forces us to make difficult choices.

We're going to make some suggestions about how to balance intrinsic and extrinsic motivation, but first we need to make an important distinction between short-term and long-term impacts on creative performance. Doing something for a reward, or doing something in the anticipation of receiving an evaluation of some sort, is likely to diminish students' creativity on whatever it is they're working on right now. Extrinsic constraints can decrease both creativity and intrinsic motivation. Over time, a steady diet of extrinsic constraints related to doing some task or studying some content is likely to lead to generally lower levels of intrinsic motivation when it comes to that task or content area.

155

Skills and knowledge can be acquired by continuing to practice or study even when one's level of intrinsic motivation is low, however, and such extrinsically motivated study may provide the very knowledge and skills one will need in the future to do something in a more creative way than would be possible at present. Similarly, the skills acquired by receiving feedback on (or evaluation of) one's performance on a task like writing an essay, constructing a mathematical proof, or designing an experiment may help one do a more competent job, and perhaps even a more creative job, on similar tasks in the future.

So perhaps we should just not worry about it; perhaps we can quiet these concerns by reminding ourselves that the skills and knowledge our students are acquiring will someday allow them to be more creative. We agree there's some truth to that idea — and although we think creativity is very important, we wouldn't argue that it's the *only* thing, or even the main thing, that schools should be doing. But we think just ignoring what we know about creativity and extrinsic and intrinsic motivation is a rather dangerous kind of burying our heads in the sand.

So what's a teacher to do? There are some things one can do, but in many cases they aren't easy. The first things we need to keep in mind are our goals or objectives for a given lesson. Sadly, we can't have it both ways, at least not at the same time: if our goal in a particular lesson is skill development or knowledge acquisition, then we need to give ourselves permission to do some things that we know make extrinsic motivation salient and depress intrinsic motivation and creativity. As much as we'd like to make *all* learning so interesting that our students would do it even without rewards or grades, no one has ever succeeded in doing that. Even the best teachers sometimes must get students to do things that some of their students don't find very interesting or enjoyable, and in those situations, we sometimes need to use rewards as bribes. We also need to provide feedback — evaluation — even if we know that this might lessen students' intrinsic interest in the task they are doing. Few of us work in a world without report cards.

On the other hand, if our goal is to encourage creativity, then we need to avoid doing things that will increase extrinsic motivation and try to do whatever we can to increase intrinsic motivation. This is just the opposite of what we sometimes need to do to teach skill and knowledge acquisition.

Some years ago John saw a cartoon about how *not* to teach for creativity. In this cartoon, a student is daydreaming some delightful and very creative things in the middle of a lesson. The student's thinking is related to the topic of the lesson, but it is clearly not the kind of thinking that is likely to produce a correct answer to the teacher's question. The teacher interrupts to remind the student that "Creativity Time" is not for another hour.

This teacher obviously didn't know much about creativity — and yet, she was doing something right (although perhaps for the wrong reason). She knew her objective for the current lesson was *not* creative thinking, and she had set aside time in which that *would* be her goal. Now we wouldn't recommend the kind of rigidity that this cartoon was depicting, but we believe that we will do a better job of both helping our students learn the content and skills they need *and* develop their creativity and their intrinsic motivation if we sometimes pursue those two different goals at different times.

What we need is a balance. This doesn't mean doing a little of both all the time — just the opposite. It means sometimes we need to go one way, and other times go the other. The trick is to make sure we are doing both, but *not* to try to do them at the same time, because when extrinsic motivation and intrinsic motivation compete, extrinsic motivation wins. If we try to combine them, what will happen most often is that intrinsic motivation, and creativity, will simply get lost in the shuffle.

Chapter 3 discussed several ways to do this and noted (in the series of "Yes, but …" qualifications) how teachers often need to alternate between creating learning environments that favor intrinsic motivators and learning environments that employ extrinsic motivators. When teaching writing, for example, we want students to learn a number of skills, and we (sometimes) want them to write imaginatively. These goals are at odds because one requires an emphasis on extrinsic motivation — evaluation, in this case — and the other requires an emphasis on intrinsic motivation, which would require us to avoid evaluation. If we try to do a little of each, it won't work, because extrinsic motivation will tend to drive out intrinsic motivation. But we *can* do both if we do them at different times. When working on skill development in writing, we can let students know that their work will be evaluated, let them know the criteria that will be applied, and then evaluate using those criteria. Other times we can tell them that although they must do the writing assignment, they'll get credit simply for doing it and there will be no further evaluation.

When you do this, you can let your students know you're looking forward to reading their stories, or whatever it is they're writing, but at the same time promise them you won't evaluate. And then keep your promise. Don't praise or criticize; don't correct or point out any errors; and don't suggest any changes, or things they might try next time. What you need to do is simply not comment at all, beyond saying that you enjoyed reading what they wrote. After a while, students will come to believe you. This will allow them, when you tell them you will be evaluating their work, to concentrate on the skills they are practicing and focus on doing things "right." It will also free them up to write more imaginatively, if with less technical correctness, during those times when you tell them that their work won't be evaluated. And this way their interest in writing won't get buried beneath a constant expectation of evaluation.

Reality check: Will some kids abuse the license that a no-evaluation promise confers? Of course they will. Let's be honest: We know that whatever we do, some kids will find (or create) cracks big enough to fall or squeeze themselves through. What we're suggesting is that sometimes we need to allow the students who want to do as little as possible to get away with it, in order not to punish those students who have the kind of intrinsic motivation that we wish all our students had.

John recalls a middle school teacher who did this one beautiful spring day. The teacher took the class outside to sketch and made it clear that students could sketch anything in any way they wanted — they could try things out, do something they thought might be interesting, or just play around with their sketches and not end up with a completed drawing — and as long as they turned something in, they would get full credit for the day's work. What did John turn in? A piece of paper with two parallel, vertical lines running from the top of the page to the bottom. When the teacher asked him to explain, he said, "it's a tree trunk, up close."

So there will be students like John was that day in art class who will abuse freedom from evaluation. But there will also be students who will use those opportunities to experiment, to take risks, and to enjoy the work they're doing in ways that they might not if grades were hanging over their heads. (And on other days, the assignments will be graded. John's art teacher didn't give him a permanent vacation from evaluation, just a temporary one.)

Will this take time away from learning content? Perhaps. But probably not as much time as one might fear. Spending a few hours each week doing content-related activities that will not be evaluated but which *will* be likely to increase students' intrinsic motivation (or at least help counter-balance the diminishment of such motivation that tends to occur in schools) won't take a large amount of time away from the kind of work we know is necessary for improving skills and acquiring content knowledge (that is, work which is evaluated so that students can use this feedback to improve their performance). And to the extent that we relate these activities to content and skills that we want students to learn, such activities may help students acquire important content knowledge and skills, even without evaluations or rewards, simply because these activities allow and encourage students to think about that content knowledge and apply those skills in different, and sometimes even original, ways.

## SUMMING UP

The goals of meeting specific content standards and of developing students' creativity are not, at least for the most part, greatly at odds. Even in an era of increasingly explicit content standards there is still room and need for teaching that encourages and endorses and enhances creative thinking. In many ways, content standards — to the extent that they result in an increase in students' fund of content knowledge and repertoire of skills — will be handmaidens to students' future creativity, and creative thinking will be an important tool in students' development of skills and acquisition of content knowledge. So we needn't stop teaching for creativity. We may, however, need to do it in more thoughtful and creative ways. By applying what creativity research has taught us about the ways teaching for creativity and teaching to acquire content knowledge are often linked — sometimes synergistically, and sometimes competitively — we can help our students both acquire more content knowledge and become more genuinely creative thinkers.

## BIBLIOGRAPHY

The "informational blotter" quote from Richard Paul comes from the 1990 book, *Critical thinking: What every person needs to survive in a rapidly changing world.* Paul was talking about one specific, content-focused curriculum, E. D. Hirsch's Core Knowledge Sequence. A few years later John did a study to test this assertion — he compared the creative performance of Core Knowledge students with that of a matched group of students who had followed that state's standard curriculum. He found that the students who had studied under the content knowledge-focused Core Knowledge curriculum actually showed *greater* creativity, not less. (That research appeared in *Creativity Research Journal* in 2003.)

The books listed at the end of Chapters 2 and 3 are the same ones we would recommend here. Readers might also be interested in James's *Creativity 101*, which is an overall summary of creativity research. John and colleagues go into more detail on these issues in a chapter in a book edited by Ron Beghetto and James, *Nurturing Creativity in the Classroom* (Cambridge, 2010). The quote from Dean Keith Simonton comes from his book *Greatness: Who Makes History and Why* (Guilford, 1994); his recent *Genius 101* (Springer, 2009) would also be of interest.

CPSIA information can be obtained at www.ICGtesting.com
Printed in the USA
BVOW020039100712

294756BV00003B/23/P